Workbook Contents

5 A

G uses of the infinitive (with *to*)
V verbs + infinitive
P word stress

I want to go to the party.

Are you a party animal?

How to survive at a party…
(when you don't know anybody!)

Has this ever happened to you? You arrive at a party or wedding reception where you don't know anybody. Everybody there seems to know each other. What can you do? Here are five simple tips.

- Don't stand in the corner. You need [1] ____to be____ positive. Find somebody you think you would like [2] _____ and go and introduce yourself.

- Try [3] _____ impersonal questions like 'I love your bag. Where did you get it?' That will help [4] _____ a conversation.

- Try [5] _____ the conversation. When you are nervous, it's very easy [6] _____ about yourself all the time. Nobody wants [7] _____ to your life story when they've only just met you.

- Smile, smile, smile. Use your body-language [8] _____ a positive, friendly impression. That way people will want [9] _____ to you.

- If you want [10] _____ from a really boring person, say that you are going to the bar [11] _____ another drink or that you need [12] _____ to the bathroom. Don't come back!

Adapted from a British magazine

1 SPEAKING

Interview a partner with the questionnaire. Ask for more information. Is your partner a 'party animal'?

Do you like going to parties? Why (not)?
Do you like giving parties? Why (not)?

When was the last time you went to a party or celebration? (for example, a wedding, a birthday party, etc.)

Whose party was it?

Did you have a good time?

What did you wear?

What kind of music did they play?

Did you dance?

Did you meet anybody new?

What did you have to eat and drink?

Did you stay until the end?

2 GRAMMAR   uses of the infinitive (with *to*)

a Read the article about parties. Complete the five rules with an infinitive.

to ask	to be	not to dominate	to escape	to get
to give	to go	to listen	to meet	to start	to talk (x2)

b Read the article again and then cover it. Can you remember the tips?

c Match the examples A–C from the text with rules 1–3.

> A It's very easy **to talk** about yourself all the time.
> B Say that you're going to the bar **to get** another drink.
> C Try **to ask** impersonal questions.

Use the infinitive (with *to*)…
1 after some verbs (e.g. *want*, *try*, etc.) ☐
2 after adjectives ☐
3 to say why you do something. ☐

d ➲ **p.134 Grammar Bank 5A.** Read the rules and do the exercises.

Clive Oxenden

Christina Latham-Koenig

Paul Seligson

FILE

e-intermediate
MultiPACK B

Page numbers in this edition are the same as
in the full-length Student's Book and Workbook.

Paul Seligson and Clive Oxenden are the original co-authors of
English File 1 (pub. 1996) and *English File 2* (pub. 1997).

OXFORD
UNIVERSITY PRESS

Student's Book Contents

Look out for Study Link This shows you where to find extra material for more practice and revision.

3 READING & LISTENING

a Read this article about the right things to say to different people at parties. In pairs, guess how to complete the **Don't say** phrases.

What to say (and what not to say) to people at parties

If you're talking to a doctor…
Don't say: I have a _____. Could you _____?
Say: You look tired. Would you like a drink?

If you're talking to a teacher…
Don't say: You're so lucky! You have _____.
Say: I'm sure it's very difficult to motivate teenagers.

If you're talking to a travel agent…
Don't say: Can you recommend _____?
Say: What's the most interesting place you've ever been to?

If you're talking to a hairdresser…
Don't say: What do you think of _____? Is it too _____?
Say: What do you think will be the new style this year?

If you're talking to a psychiatrist…
Don't say: Are you _____?
Say: Do you work with children or adults?

b 5.1 Now listen to some people at a party who say the wrong things. Complete the **Don't say** phrases. Did you guess any of them?

c Listen to the people at the party again. Complete the conversations with an infinitive.

Conversation 1	I want _____ _____ him a 'Happy Birthday'.
Conversation 2	Perhaps you would like _____ _____ my class one day.
Conversation 3	I'd like _____ _____ somewhere _____.
Conversation 4	You're just the person I want _____ _____ to.
Conversation 5	I need _____ _____ to the _____.

4 VOCABULARY   verbs + infinitive

a ➲ p.154 Vocabulary Bank *Verb forms* (Verb + infinitive). Look at some other verbs followed by the infinitive. Highlight any that you didn't know.

b ➲ **Communication** *Guess the infinitive A p.110 B p.114.*

5 PRONUNCIATION & SPEAKING

⚠ Two- and three-syllable words usually have the stress on the first syllable. Always underline the stress in new words.

a In pairs underline the stressed syllable in these words.

dangerous	decide	difficult	forget	important
interesting	possible	pretend	promise	remember

b 5.2 Listen and check. Practise saying the words.

c Choose five questions and ask a partner.

Do you find it **difficult to remember** people's names?

Do you think it's **important to learn** to cook?

What's the most **interesting place to visit** in your town?

Have you ever **forgotten to turn off** your mobile in a cinema or a concert?

Do you think it's **possible to learn** a foreign language without going to the country?

Is there any part of your town where it's **dangerous to go** at night?

Do you always **remember to phone** your friends on their birthdays?

When was the last time you **promised not to come** home late?

Have you ever **pretended to be** ill (when you weren't)?

Have you **decided to go** anywhere next summer?

5 B

G verb + *-ing*
V verbs followed by *-ing*
P *-ing*

I love waking up on a sunny morning.

What makes you feel good?

We asked readers from all over the world to tell us what makes them feel good

- Eating outside. I love sitting at street cafés or having meals in the garden, even when the weather's not perfect – which it often isn't.

- Being with people I like (and not being with people I don't like).

- Sitting on a plane when it takes off – you can't control what's going to happen for the next 2–3 hours so you can really relax.

- Waking up on a sunny morning during my holidays when I know I have a whole day ahead to do the things I really like doing.

- Getting out of the city. It doesn't matter where to, to the beach, or to the country, or to the forest. Being in the middle of nature makes me feel alive.

- Watching heavy rain storms through the window from a comfortable, warm room with a fire, and knowing I don't need to go out.

- Talking to intelligent people: good conversation is one of life's great pleasures.

- Having time for myself. Unfortunately, it doesn't happen very often.

- Reading books or magazines in English – I'm Hungarian, and I still find it hard to believe that I can enjoy reading without using a dictionary in a language that once was a complete mystery.

- Tidying a cupboard. It stops me from thinking about my problems.

1 READING

a Read the article once. How many people mention...?
1 the weather
2 holidays and travelling
3 housework
4 nature
5 other people

b Read the article again and tick (✓) the *three* things you agree with most. Then put a cross (✗) next to any you don't agree with. Compare with a partner. Say why.

c Underline five new words or phrases you want to learn from the text.

2 GRAMMAR verb + *-ing*

A Being with people I like (makes me feel good).
B I love sitting at cafés...
C I can enjoy reading without using a dictionary.

a Match sentences A–C with rules 1–3.

Use the *-ing* form…
1 after some verbs (e.g. *like, love*, etc.) ☐
2 when we use a verb as a noun (e.g. as the subject of a sentence) ☐
3 when we use a verb after a preposition ☐

b Look at the highlighted verbs. Can you remember the spelling rules for making the *-ing* form?

c ➲ **p.134 Grammar Bank 5B.** Read the rules and do the exercises.

d Now write two things that make *you* feel good (that are not in the article). Compare with a partner.

3 PRONUNCIATION -ing

a **5.3** Listen and repeat the sound picture
   and the words.

thing	bring wrong language
	sitting watching thanks think

b ⭕ **p.159 Sound Bank.** Look at the typical spellings
   for this sound.

> ⚠ When we add -ing /ɪŋ/ to a verb, the pronunciation
> of the original verb doesn't change.
> *do* /duː/ → *doing* /ˈduːwɪŋ/
> *forget* → *forgetting*

c **5.4** Listen and say the -ing form of the verbs
   you hear.

4 VOCABULARY & SPEAKING

a ⭕ **p.154 Vocabulary Bank** *Verb forms* (Verb + -ing).
   Look at other verbs which are followed by the
   -ing form.

b Work in pairs. Choose five things to talk about
   from the list below.

> a job you **don't mind** doing in the house
> a sport you **enjoy** watching
> something you **like** doing with your family
> something you **love** doing in the summer
> something you **hate** doing at work / school
> something you **spend** a lot of time doing
> somebody you **dream of** meeting
> something you **don't like** doing alone
> a country you are **interested in** visiting
> something you are **thinking of** doing this weekend
> something you have **stopped** doing
> something you are not very **good at** doing

c A tell B about the five things. Say why. B ask for
   more information. Then swap roles.

> I don't mind cooking. It's quite relaxing.

> Do you cook every day?

5 LISTENING

a Ask and answer these questions in pairs.

> Do you ever sing…?
> in the shower
> in the car
> at karaoke bars
> while you're listening to a CD
> in a choir /kwaɪə/ or a band

b In pairs, say if you think sentences 1–7 are T (true)
   or F (false).
   1 Singing is good for your health.
   2 To sing well you need to learn to breathe correctly.
   3 People who sing are fatter than people who don't.
   4 Not everybody can learn to sing.
   5 You need to know how to read music to be able to sing well.
   6 If you make a surprised face, you can sing high notes better.
   7 It takes a long time to learn to sing better.

c **5.5** Now listen to an interview with the director
   of a singing school and a student who did a course there.
   Were you right?

d Listen again. Choose the right answer.

   1 When you are learning to sing you need to _____ correctly.
      a stand   **b** dress   **c** eat
   2 Singing well·is 95% _____.
      a repeating   **b** listening   **c** breathing
   3 Gemma's course lasted _____.
      a one day   **b** one week   **c** one month
   4 Gemma has always _____.
      a been good at singing   **b** been in a choir   **c** liked singing
   5 In the morning the students learnt to _____.
      a breathe and sing   **b** listen and breathe   **c** listen and sing
   6 At the end of the afternoon they could sing _____.
      a perfectly   **b** much better   **c** a bit better

5 C

G *have to, don't have to, must, mustn't*
V modifiers: *a bit, really*, etc.
P sentence stress

> You have to come to all the classes.
> You don't have to do an exam.

How much can you learn in a month?

1 GRAMMAR *have to, don't have to, must, mustn't*

a Look at these notices. Have you seen any like these in your school?

A
SILENCE
Exam
in progress

B
Tonight's film:
***Pirates of the
Caribbean***
Entrance free

C
Course fees
to be paid
in advance

D

E No food here please

F Extra pronunciation class
5pm

b Match the notices with the rules.

1 You have to pay before you start. ☐
2 You don't have to come if you don't want to. ☐
3 You mustn't eat in here. ☐
4 You must turn off your mobiles before you come in. ☐
5 You mustn't talk near here. ☐
6 You don't have to pay to see this. ☐

c Look at the highlighted expressions and answer the questions.

1 Which two phrases mean…?
It is a rule. There's an obligation to do this.   *You have to*
    _____

2 Which phrase means…?
It isn't obligatory. It isn't necessary.   _____
3 Which phrase means…?
It isn't permitted. It is against the rules.   _____

d ⟳ **p.134 Grammar Bank 5C.** Read the rules and do the exercises.

2 PRONUNCIATION sentence stress

a (5.6) Listen and write the six sentences.

b Listen again and repeat the sentences. Copy the rhythm. Which
letter is 'silent' in *mustn't*?

c Make true sentences about the rules in the school where you are
studying English. Use *We have to*, *We don't have to*, or *We mustn't*.

1 _____ come to lessons on time.
2 _____ turn off our mobile phones.
3 _____ eat or drink in the classroom.
4 _____ come to class on Saturday.
5 _____ bring a dictionary to class.
6 _____ do an exam at the end of the year.
7 _____ smoke in the building.
8 _____ do homework after each lesson.
9 _____ do a test every week.

3 READING & LISTENING

a Do you think people from your country
are good at learning languages? Why (not)?

b Read about Anna, a British journalist who
did an intensive Polish course. Then cover
the article and answer the questions.

1 What languages did Anna already know?
2 Why did she choose to learn Polish?
3 Where did she do the course?
4 What did she think was the most difficult
thing about Polish?
5 Where is she going to do the 'tests'?
6 What five things does she have to do?
7 What are the rules?

Anna in Kraków

How much can you learn in a month?

I work for a magazine, which was doing an article about British language learners. As an experiment, they asked me to learn a completely new language for one month. Then I had to go to the country and do some 'tests' to see if I could 'survive' in different situations. I decided to learn Polish because my great-grandmother was Polish and I have some relatives there. I can already speak French and Spanish quite well but Polish isn't a Latin-based language so I knew it would be completely different.

I did a one-month intensive course at a language school in Birmingham. I thought I was good at languages before I started learning Polish, but now I'm not so sure. I found it incredibly difficult. The grammar was really complicated and the words were not like any other language I know so it was very hard to remember them. For example, I thought 'football' was more or less an international word, but in Polish it's *piłka nożna*. And the pronunciation is unbelievable! Every word is full of z's where you don't expect them, like *jeździsz* which means 'you go'.

My course finished yesterday and I'm going to Kraków for the weekend to do my tests. A local guide called Kasia is coming with me and is going to give me a mark out of 10.

These are the tests and the rules:

> ### Tests
> You have to…
> 1 get a taxi.
> 2 order a drink in a bar.
> 3 ask for directions (and follow them).
> 4 phone and ask to speak to someone.
> 5 ask somebody the time.
>
> ### Rules
> – you mustn't use a dictionary or phrasebook.
> – you mustn't speak English at any time.
> – you mustn't use your hands or mime.

c **5.7** Which test do you think will be the easiest for Anna? Which will be the most difficult? Listen to Anna doing the tests in Kraków and check your answers.

d Listen again. Mark the sentences T (true) or F (false). Correct the false ones.
1 The taxi driver couldn't speak English.
2 Anna understood the waitress's question.
3 She ordered a small Coke.
4 Anna asked for directions to a bank.
5 She couldn't understand what the woman said.
6 Anna couldn't understand everything the woman on the phone said.
7 Anna thought telling the time in Polish was very easy.
8 She didn't find out what the time was.
9 Kasia gave her eight out of ten for her Polish.

4 SPEAKING

a How well could you do Anna's five tests in English? How much do you think you can learn in a month?

b Talk to a partner.

> **Have you ever…**
> spoken in English on the phone? Who to? What about?
> seen a film in English? Which? How much did you understand?
> spoken to a tourist in English? When? Why?
> read an English book or magazine? Which ones?
> asked for directions in a foreign city? Where? What happened?
> learnt another foreign language? How well can you speak it?

5 VOCABULARY modifiers

> I found Polish **incredibly** difficult.
> I felt **a bit** stupid when the taxi driver spoke perfect English.

a Complete the chart with the words in the box.

a bit	incredibly	~~not very~~	quite	really	~~very~~

Polish is | very | difficult

not very

b Complete the sentences with one of the words so they are true for you. Compare with a partner.
1 I'm _____ good at learning languages.
2 I'm _____ motivated to improve my English.
3 English pronunciation is _____ difficult.
4 English grammar is _____ complicated.
5 I'm _____ worried about the next English exam.
6 English is _____ useful for my work / studies.

G expressing movement
V prepositions of movement, sport
P prepositions

The name of the game

> The ball went over the net.

1 VOCABULARY & SPEAKING
sport, prepositions of movement

a Look at the photos. Can you name the sports?
Write them in the correct column.

play	go	do

b **5.8** Listen and check.

c In pairs, say…
Which of the sports in **a** are usually team sports?
How many **players** are there?
In which sports do you…?
a **hit** the ball   b **throw** the ball   c **kick** the ball   d **shoot**

d Ask and answer with a partner.

Do you do any sports? Which one(s)?
Which sports do you enjoy watching?
Which sports do you hate watching?
Are you (or anyone in your family) a fan of a sports team?
  Which one?
Do you (or they) watch their matches? Where?

e Where did the ball go? Complete with a preposition.

across	along	down	into	~~over~~

The ball went ___*over*___ the wall, _____ the street, _____
the steps, _____ the road, and _____ the river.

f ⭢ **p.148 Vocabulary Bank** *Prepositions.* Do part 2.

2 GRAMMAR expressing movement

The rules of the game

1 You play this sport outside with one, two, or more players. You have to hit the ball into a small hole. You mustn't hit the ball into the water.

2 You can play this sport outside or inside with two or four players. You have to hit the ball over a net and the ball mustn't go 'out'.

3 You usually do this sport outside (but it can be inside). You have to go round a track many times and be the first one to go past the finish line. Sometimes you have to go round a country, for example, France.

4 You play this sport outside with two teams. You have to pass the ball to other players with your foot and try to kick the ball into the goal. You mustn't touch the ball with your hands.

5 You play this sport outside with two teams. You have to throw the ball to other players and take the ball over the other team's line. You can also get points by kicking the ball through two very high posts.

a Match the rules to the sports in 1. What are the sports?

b **5.9** Listen and check.

c Look at the sports rules again and the highlighted words. How do you express movement in English?

d ⭢ **p.134 Grammar Bank 5D.** Read the rules and do the exercises.

3 PRONUNCIATION prepositions

a Match the prepositions with the phonetics. How do you pronounce the words?

across	along	into	over
round	through	towards	

1 /ˈɪntuː/ _____
2 /əˈlɒŋ/ _____
3 /raʊnd/ _____
4 /təˈwɔːdz/ _____
5 /əˈkrɒs/ _____
6 /θruː/ _____
7 /ˈəʊvə/ _____

b **5.10** Listen and check. <u>Underline</u> the stressed syllable, and practise saying the prepositions.

c ➲ **Communication** *Cross country p.117.* Tell your partner where the runner went.

4 READING & SPEAKING

a How long does a normal football match last? How many minutes are added after each half?

b Read the article and complete it with a word from below.

champions	fans	goal	~~match~~	pitch
players	referee	scored	stadium	team

c Read the text again. Number the sentences 1–6.

A Manchester United scored their first goal. ☐
B The Bayern Munich fans started celebrating. ☐
C The 90 minutes finished and the referee added three minutes. ☐
D Bayern Munich scored a goal. 1
E Manchester United scored their second goal. ☐
F The UEFA president left his seat to go to present the cup. ☐

d What is the most exciting sporting event you've ever seen? Prepare your answers to these questions.

1 What sport was it?
2 When and where was it?
3 Who was taking part?
4 Were you there or did you see it on TV?
5 What happened?

e Ask and answer with a partner.

5 **5.11** SONG ♫ *We are the champions*

Your most exciting sporting moments...

This week, Duc from Vietnam writes:

The most exciting football [1] __*match*__ I have ever seen was the 1999 Champions' League Final between Manchester United and Bayern Munich in the Nou Camp [2] _____ in Barcelona.

After 90 minutes Manchester United were losing 1–0. The Bayern Munich [3] _____ in the stadium were already celebrating their [4] _____'s victory. The Manchester United fans in the stadium and millions around the world were watching in despair.

There were now just three minutes of added time. 20 seconds passed and United got a corner. The atmosphere in the stadium was incredibly intense. All the Manchester United [5] _____ (including their goalkeeper) were in the Bayern Munich penalty area. David Beckham took the corner and Teddy Sheringham [6] _____. It was 1–1!

The Manchester United fans were ecstatic. There was only about one minute left now but United attacked again and scored another [7] _____. Now it was 2–1! 30 seconds later we heard the [8] _____ blow his whistle. The match was over. United were the [9] _____! Many of the Bayern fans and players were crying. They had lost the match in less than three minutes.

The next day I read that the UEFA president missed both Manchester United's goals. He was going down to the [10] _____ to give the cup to the German team when United scored their first goal and he was going back up to his seat when they scored their second! He missed the most exciting and unforgettable three minutes of football I have ever seen.

5 At a department store PRACTICAL ENGLISH

BUYING CLOTHES

5.12 Listen to Allie shopping. Answer the questions.

1 What does Allie want to buy?
2 What size is she?
3 Does she try it on?
4 How much does Allie think it costs?
5 How does she pay?

TAKING SOMETHING BACK

a **5.13** Cover the dialogue and listen. What's the problem with Allie's sweater? Does she change it or ask for her money back?

YOU HEAR	YOU SAY
Can I help you?	Yes, I bought this sweater about half an hour ago.
Yes, I remember. Is there a _____?	Yes, I've decided it's too big for me.
What _____ is it?	Medium.
So you need a _____. I don't see one here.	Do you have any more?
I'll go and check. Just a _____.	
I'm sorry but we don't have _____ one in black.	Oh dear.
We can order one for you. It'll only take a few _____.	No, I'm leaving on Saturday.
Would you like to exchange it for _____ else?	Not really. Could I have a refund?
No problem. Do you _____ the receipt?	Yes, here you are.

b Listen again. Complete the **YOU HEAR** phrases.

c **5.14** Listen and repeat the **YOU SAY** phrases. Copy the <u>rhythm</u>.

d In pairs, roleplay the dialogue. **A** (book open) you're the shop assistant, **B** (book closed) you're Allie. Swap roles.

SOCIAL ENGLISH the conference cocktail party

a **5.15** Listen and complete with *Mark*, *Allie*, or *Brad*.

1 _Allie_ tells _____ about the shopping and museum.
2 _____ comes to say hello to _____ and _____.
3 _____ is surprised that _____ and _____ met this morning.
4 _____ asks _____ if she wants a drink.
5 _____ is annoyed, but goes to get the drinks.

b Complete the USEFUL PHRASES, Listen again and check.

c **5.16** Listen and repeat the phrases. How do you say them in your language?

USEFUL PHRASES
M What did you t_____ of it?
A Never m_____.
A What a l_____ evening!
A I got l_____.
M What would you like to d_____?
B What a good i_____.

a Read the e-mail to a language school. Tick (✓) the questions that Adriano wants the school to answer.

☐ How much do the courses cost?
☐ When do the courses start and finish?
☐ How many students are there in a class?
☐ Are there Business English classes?
☐ Where can I stay?
☐ Where are the teachers from?

b Look at the highlighted expressions. How would they be different in an informal e-mail (or letter)?

Formal e-mail	Informal e-mail
Dear Sir / Madam	_____
I am writing	
I would like	
I look forward to hearing from you	
Yours faithfully	

From: Adriano Ruocco [adrianor@tiscali.net]

To: The Grange Language School [enquiries@grangeedinburgh]
Subject: Information about courses

Dear Sir / Madam ,

I am writing to ask for information about your language courses. I am especially interested in an intensive course of two or three weeks. I am 31 and I work in the library at Milan University. I can read English quite well but I need to improve my listening and speaking. The book I am currently studying is 'pre-intermediate' (Common European Framework level A2).

I have looked at your website, but there is no information about intensive courses next summer. Could you please send me information about dates and prices? I would also like some information about accommodation. If possible I would like to stay with a family. My wife is going to visit me for a weekend when I am at the school. Could she stay with me in the same family?

I look forward to hearing from you.

Yours faithfully

Adriano Ruocco

---

c Read the advertisements and choose a course. Think of two or three questions you would like to ask.

Thai Cookery courses in Chiang Mai

Learn to cook Thai food in northern Thailand. One week courses, from April to October. Your accommodation in Chiang Mai is included. Beginners welcome. E-mail us for more information at thaicook@blueelephant.com

Tennis courses in France

One- or two-week courses in different parts of the country. Professional tennis coaches. All levels, beginners to advanced. Small groups or private lessons. For more information e-mail us at info@tennisinfrance.com

---

WRITE a formal e-mail asking for information. Write two paragraphs.

Paragraph 1 Explain why you are writing and give some personal information.

Paragraph 2 Ask your questions, and ask them to send you information.

CHECK your e-mail for mistakes (grammar , punctuation , and spelling).

GRAMMAR

Circle the correct answer, a, b, or c.

What's _____ name?

a yours (b) your c you

1 We want _____ a party next month.
  a have
  b to have
  c having

2 It's often difficult _____ new friends.
  a to make
  b make
  c for make

3 She bought a new dress _____ at the party.
  a for to wear
  b for wear
  c to wear

4 _____ early on a sunny morning makes me feel good.
  a Waking up
  b Wake up
  c To wake up

5 My brother doesn't enjoy _____ by plane.
  a travel
  b to travel
  c travelling

6 I'm tired of _____ TV. Let's do something different.
  a to watch
  b watching
  c watch

7 I like Saturdays because I _____ work.
  a mustn't
  b don't have to
  c haven't to

8 She can't come to the cinema because she _____ to study.
  a must
  b have
  c has

9 You _____ be late for class tomorrow. You have an exam.
  a mustn't
  b mustn't to
  c don't must

10 The golf ball _____ the hill and into the river.
  a down
  b downed
  c went down

10

VOCABULARY

a verb phrases

Complete the sentences.

I don't _enjoy_ going to parties.

decide	dream of	forget	hate	hope	learn	mind	need	start	try

1 **A** Which film do you want to see? **B** I don't _____. You choose.
2 Don't _____ to buy some milk at the supermarket.
3 I _____ finding the perfect job.
4 Your hair's very long. You _____ to go to the hairdresser's.
5 What did you _____? Are you coming or not?
6 I'd like to _____ to play chess. Can you teach me?
7 I always travel by train or car because I _____ flying.
8 I _____ to see you soon.
9 _____ to read in English as much as you can.
10 Don't _____ running until you hear 'Go'.

b prepositions of movement

Complete the sentences with a preposition.

In the 100 metres race the athletes have to run _along_ a track.

1 In golf you have to hit the ball _____ the hole.
2 In tennis you have to hit the ball _____ the net.
3 In football you have to pass the ball _____ the other players on your team.
4 In Formula 1 you have to drive _____ a track.
5 In rugby you have to kick the ball _____ the posts.

c sport verbs

Complete the sentences with *play*, *do*, and *go* in the correct form.

1 We _____ football every Saturday.
2 I _____ skiing last year.
3 He _____ judo twice a week.
4 She often _____ cycling after work.
5 They love _____ aerobics.

20

PRONUNCIATION

a Underline the word with a different sound

1		hit	mind	kick	finish
2		promise	like	decide	tired
3	ei	hate	have	game	race
4	aʊ	out	round	down	throw
5	uː	through	mustn't	doing	music

b Underline the stressed syllable.

information

promise	decide	forget	enjoy	practise

10

CAN YOU UNDERSTAND THIS TEXT?

a Read the article. Is Alexandra Kosteniuk...?

1 beautiful but not very good at chess.

2 not very beautiful but good at chess.

3 beautiful and good at chess.

b Read the article again and mark the sentences T (true), F (false), or DS (doesn't say).

1 The International Chess Federation wants chess to have a more modern image.

2 Alexandra never wears glasses.

3 Alexandra's father taught her to play chess.

4 She became a grandmaster after playing chess for five years.

5 She thinks that chess should be more popular.

6 If you have Internet access, you can play chess with Alexandra.

7 Nigel Short has an attractive personality.

The new face of chess

17-year-old Alexandra Kosteniuk is sometimes called the Anna Kournikova of the chess world. The International Chess Federation have asked her to be the new face of the game, which traditionally has had an image of middle-aged men wearing glasses.

Alexandra started playing chess when she was five. She learnt to play from her father, and became a grandmaster when she was only 14. Experts say that her game is one of the most exciting they have seen for a long time.

'Chess is not as popular as it should be, and I think I could help it,' Kosteniuk said last week. 'It is an honour for me to be described as the face of the game.' She has her own website with pictures, poems, and the opportunity to play chess against her.

Making the game faster is another part of the campaign to make chess more popular. There are now strict time limits for making moves. Games that before lasted for hours can now take place in five minutes. The longest international tournament games, which sometimes took days, now last only four to seven hours.

Nigel Short, the British grandmaster, says, 'There are a lot of attractive women in chess, but Alexandra Kosteniuk has made a very big impression. She is obviously very talented. Any sport needs attractive personalities, and I have no problem with marketing the game through her.'

Adapted from a British newspaper

CAN YOU UNDERSTAND THESE PEOPLE?

a **5.17** Listen to five short conversations. Circle a, b, or c.

1 Anna _____ to go to the party.
   a wants   b doesn't want   c isn't sure if she wants

2 The concert was _____.
   a awful   b quite good   c very good

3 Maria is _____ late for class.
   a never   b hardly ever   c often

4 The woman speaks _____ very well.
   a French   b German   c Italian

5 Henry kicked the ball _____.
   a into the goal   b over the top of the goal   c to the left of the goal

b **5.18** Listen and complete the form for the Milford Sports Centre.

Sport: ¹ _____   Day: ² _____

Time: from ³ _____   to ⁴ _____

Name: ⁵ _____   Cost: ⁶ _____

CAN YOU SAY THIS IN ENGLISH?

a Can you...? Yes (✓)

☐ talk about the last party you went to

☐ talk about what makes you feel good and why

☐ say what you have to do to learn a language

☐ describe the rules for a sport you know

b Complete the questions with a verb in the *-ing* form or infinitive.

1 Where do you want _____ for your next holiday?

2 Have you ever tried to learn _____? What happened?

3 Do you enjoy _____? Why (not)?

4 Do you have to _____ at work / school?

5 What sport would you like _____?

c Ask your partner the questions in **b**. Ask for more information.

63

6 A

G *if* + present, *will* + infinitive (first conditional)
V confusing verbs
P long and short vowels

> If you change queues,
> the other one will move faster.

If something bad can happen, it will

1 GRAMMAR *if* + present, *will* + infinitive

a Read the beginning of the story. Why do you think the Italian doesn't want to lend his newspaper to the American?

Murder on the Orient Express?

A young American was travelling to Venice on the Orient Express. It was a long journey, and he was bored. Sitting opposite him there was an Italian man. He was about 50 years old. He had an English newspaper on the seat next to him.

'Excuse me,' the American said. 'Can I borrow your newspaper?'

'No,' said the Italian. 'I'm sorry. You can't.'

'Why not?' asked the American.

'Well,' said the Italian, 'it's quite simple...'

b Look at the pictures. Number the rest of the story 1–9.

- ☐ 'If you meet Nicoletta, you'll fall in love with her.'
- ☐ 'If we start talking, we'll become friends.'
- ☐ 'If I invite you to my house, you'll meet my beautiful daughter, Nicoletta.'
- ☐ 'So that's why I won't lend you my newspaper.'
- ☐ 'If I find you, I'll kill you.'
- ☐ 'If you fall in love with her, you'll run away together.'
- ☐ 'If we become friends, I'll invite you to my house in Venice.'
- 1 'If I lend you my newspaper, we'll start talking.'
- ☐ 'If you run away, I'll find you.'

c 🔊 **6.1** Listen and check. Then cover sentences 1–9 and look at the pictures. Try to remember the sentences.

d Look at the sentences again. What tense is the verb after *if*? What tense is the other verb?

e ➡ **p.136 Grammar Bank 6A.** Read the rules and do the exercises.

2 VOCABULARY confusing verbs

a What's the difference between *know* and *meet*, and *borrow* and *lend*? Underline the right verb.

1 You'll **know** / **meet** my beautiful daughter Nicoletta.
2 Do you **know** / **meet** my sister's boyfriend?
3 Can I **borrow** / **lend** your newspaper?
4 If I **borrow** / **lend** you my newspaper, we'll start talking.

b ➡ **p.149 Vocabulary Bank** *Verbs*. Do part 2.

3 READING

a If you are in a supermarket and you change queues, what will happen?

b Read the first paragraph of the article *Murphy's Law*. Who was Murphy? What exactly is his law?

c Read the rest of the article. Can you guess how the examples 1–8 of Murphy's Law finish?

Murphy's Law

If you change queues in a supermarket, what will happen? The queue you were in before will move more quickly. You know what will happen, because there's a law of life that says, 'if something bad can happen, it will happen'. It's called Murphy's Law, and it took its name from Captain Edward Murphy, an American aeroplane engineer from the 1940s. He was investigating why planes crashed, and not surprisingly, he got a reputation for always thinking of the worst thing that can happen in every situation...

At home

1 If you wash your car,... ☐
2 If you look for something you've lost,... ☐

Social life

3 If you wear something white,... ☐
4 If someone near you is smoking,... ☐

Shopping

5 If you find something in a shop that you really like,... ☐
6 If you take something that doesn't work back to a shop,... ☐

Transport

7 If you stop waiting for a bus and start walking,... ☐
8 If you get to the station and a train is just leaving,... ☐

d Now match them with A–H from the box below.

> A you'll spill wine or coffee on it.
> B it'll rain.
> C they won't have it in your size.
> D it'll be your train.
> E the bus will come.
> F it'll start working.
> G you'll find it in the last place you look.
> H the smoke will always go directly towards you.

e In pairs, look only at the first half of the sentences in the text. How many of the 'laws' can you remember? Can you think of any others?

4 PRONUNCIATION long and short vowels

a **6.2** Listen and repeat the pairs of long and short vowels. Practise making the difference.

b Put these words into the chart.

beautiful	borrow	if	law	leave	look
meet	move	push	queue	stop	story
talk	took	wash	we'll	will	win

c **6.3** Listen and check. Practise saying the words.

d **→ p.157 Sound Bank.** Look at the typical spellings for these sounds.

5 SPEAKING

In pairs or small groups, invent some new 'Murphy's Laws' beginning with the sentence halves below.

If you're single and you meet somebody you really like,...

If you throw something away,...

If you park a long way from where you're going,...

If your baby goes to sleep late,...

If you're driving somewhere and you're in a hurry,...

If you arrive very early to catch a plane,...

If you get to work late,...

If you leave your mobile phone at home,...

If you push a door,...

6 B

G *if* + past, *would* + infinitive (second conditional)
V animals
P stress and rhythm

> If I saw a bear, I'd run away.

Never smile at a crocodile

Would *you* survive?

We all enjoy seeing wild animals on the television. But what would happen if we met one in real life? Do our animal quiz and see if you would survive.

1 What would you do ...

... if you were in the middle of a river and suddenly you saw a crocodile swimming quickly towards you?

a I would try to swim to the bank as quickly as possible. ☐
b I wouldn't move. I'd stay still and wait for the crocodile to go away. ☐
c I would try to hit the crocodile in the face. ☐

2 What would you do ...

... if you were in a forest and a very large bear came towards you?

a I would climb up the nearest tree. ☐
b I would lie on the ground and pretend to be dead. ☐
c I would run away as fast as I could. ☐

3 What would you do ...

... if you were in the middle of a field and a bull started running towards you?

a I would run. ☐
b I would throw something (e.g. my hat) in another direction. ☐
c I would shout and wave my arms. ☐

1 SPEAKING & LISTENING

a Read the quiz and tick (✓) your answers, **a**, **b**, or **c**. Compare with a partner.

b (6.4) Now listen to a survival expert. Did you choose the right answer?

c Listen again. Why are the other two answers wrong? Compare what you heard with a partner.

2 GRAMMAR *if* + past, *would* + infinitive

a Look at question 1 in *Would you survive?* and answer these questions.

1 Is the crocodile situation...?
   a one which could easily happen to you
   OR
   b one which is not very probable.
2 What tense of the verb goes after *if*?
3 What's the form of the other verbs in the question and in the answers?

b ❍ **p.136 Grammar Bank 6B.** Read the rules and do the exercises.

3 PRONUNCIATION stress and rhythm

a (6.5) Listen and repeat the sentence halves and then the whole sentence. Copy the rhythm.

1 If I <u>saw</u> a <u>crocodile</u>,   I'd <u>climb</u> a <u>tree</u>.
2 What would you <u>do</u>   if you <u>saw</u> a <u>snake</u>?
3 We could <u>have</u> a <u>dog</u>   if we <u>had</u> a <u>garden</u>.
4 If a <u>bear</u> <u>attacked</u> me,   I <u>wouldn't</u> <u>move</u>.
5 If <u>I</u> were <u>you</u>,   I'd <u>go</u> on a <u>safari</u>.

b Cover the right-hand column. Try to remember the sentences.

4 VOCABULARY animals

a Answer the questions with a partner.

1 Do (or did you) have a pet? What?
2 What's the most dangerous animal in your country?
3 What's your favourite film about an animal?
4 What's your favourite cartoon animal?
5 If you went on a safari, what animal would you most like to see?
6 Are there any animals or insects you are really afraid of?
7 If you were an animal, what would you like to be?

b ➲ **p.151 Vocabulary Bank** *Animals*.

c **6.6** Listen. Which animal can you hear?

5 SPEAKING

Choose five questions and ask your partner.

What would you do...

... if there was a mouse in your bedroom?
... if you were driving and a bee or a wasp came into the car?
... if you saw a spider in the bath?
... if you were on a beach that was famous for shark attacks?
... if someone offered to buy you a fur coat?
... if you went to your friends' house for dinner and they gave you horse meat?
... if your neighbour's dog barked all night?
... if a friend asked you to look after their cat or dog?

6 READING

a Can you remember the best way to survive a crocodile attack?

b Read the article about crocodiles and mark the sentences T (true), F (false), or DS (doesn't say).

1 The Australian crocodile is bigger than all other kinds.
2 Crocodiles can run faster than horses.
3 Crocodiles only attack you if you are in the water.
4 The German tourist didn't know that there might be crocodiles in the lake.
5 The crocodile also attacked the girl's friends.
6 The Australian boy was killed when he and his friends went swimming in a river.
7 His friends escaped by climbing a tree.
8 Norman Pascoe's aunt was attacked by a crocodile.
9 She hit it on the nose, and it opened its mouth.

NATURE'S PERFECT KILLING MACHINE

THE AUSTRALIAN CROCODILE is the largest crocodile in the world. It can grow up to seven metres long and the biggest can weigh up to 1000 kilos. It has only two muscles to open its mouth but 40 to close it!

What makes crocodiles so dangerous is that they attack incredibly quickly and they take their victims under the water to drown them. They usually attack in the water, but they can suddenly come out of a river and attack animals or people, and they can run on land at 17 km/h.

Every year in Australia there are crocodile attacks on humans. Two years ago a 24-year-old German tourist died when she went for a swim in a lake. Although there were signs warning people that there might be crocodiles, the girl and her friends decided to have a midnight swim. The girl suddenly disappeared and next morning her body was found. Near it was a four-metre crocodile. And only last month two Australian boys watched in horror as their friend was killed by a crocodile when they were washing their mountain bikes in a river. They climbed a tree and stayed there for 22 hours while the crocodile waited below.

But you CAN survive a crocodile attack. Last year Norman Pascoe, a 19-year-old, was saved from a crocodile when his aunt hit it on the nose. Norman's aunt said: 'I hit it and I shouted, "Help!" The crocodile suddenly opened its mouth and my nephew escaped.'

Adapted from a British newspaper

c Cover the text. In pairs, can you remember what these numbers refer to?

| 7 | 1000 | 40 | 17 | 24 | 22 | 19 |

d Read the text again and check your answers.

7 **6.7** SONG ♫ *Wouldn't it be nice*

G may / might (possibility)
V word building: noun formation
P sentence stress, -ion endings

I might go, but I might not.

Decisions, decisions

1 SPEAKING

a Complete the definitions with words from the box. Underline the stressed syllable.

decision	decisive	indecisive	decide

1 _____ /dɪˈsaɪd/ *verb* think about two or more possibilities and choose one

2 _____ /dɪˈsɪʒn/ *noun* from 1

3 _____ /dɪˈsaɪsɪv/ *adj* good at making decisions

4 _____ /ɪndɪˈsaɪsɪv/ *adj* not good at making decisions

b Interview your partner with the questionnaire. Ask for more information. Which of you is more indecisive?

Are you indecisive?

	Yes	No	Sometimes
Do you find it difficult to make decisions?			
Do you have problems deciding…			
– what to wear when you go out?			
– what to eat in a restaurant?			
– what to do in your free time?			
– where to go on holiday?			
– what to buy when you go shopping?			
Do you often change your mind about something?			
Do you think you are indecisive?			

Yes   No   I'm not sure

2 GRAMMAR may / might

a 6.8 Cover the dialogue and listen. Who's indecisive, Roz or Mel? What about?

R Hi Mel. It's me... Roz.

M Hi Roz.

R Listen Mel. It's about the party tonight.

M You're going, aren't you?

R I don't know. I'm not sure. I might _____ but I might not. I can't decide.

M Oh come on. You'll love it. And you might _____ somebody new.

R OK. I'll go then.

M Good. So what are you going to wear?

R That's the other problem. I'm not sure what to wear. I might _____ my new black trousers. Or perhaps the red dress – what do you think?

M If I were you, I'd wear the red dress.

R But the red dress may _____ too small for me now…

M Well, wear the black trousers then.

R OK. I'll wear the black trousers.

M How are you getting there?

R I might _____ with John… or Ruth… or I may _____ there… I'm not sure yet.

M OK, I'll see you there. Bye.

R Bye.

M Hello?

R Mel? It's me again. Roz. Listen. I've changed my mind. Sorry. I'm not going to go to the party.

b Listen again and complete the conversation.

c Underline the verb phrases in the dialogue with *may / might*. Do we use them for…?

1 an obligation   OR   2 a possibility

d ➲ **p.136 Grammar Bank 6C.** Read the rules and do the exercises.

3 PRONUNCIATION & SPEAKING

a **6.9** Listen and repeat the *may* / *might* phrases from the dialogue. Copy the rhythm. Are *may* and *might* stressed?

b ○ **Communication** *Decisions, decisions A p.110 B p.115.* In pairs, roleplay being indecisive.

4 READING

a You're going to read some tips to help people to make decisions. Before you read, cover the text. In pairs, try to predict what one of the tips will be.

b Quickly look through the article. Is your tip there? Then complete the text with these verbs from the box.

> ask   compare   confuse   feel   have
> make (x2)   ~~take~~   use   wait

c Read the article again. In pairs, try to decide which tip is the best. Can you think of one other tip?

How to make decisions
When you have to choose between two possibilities:

- ¹ __*Take*__ your time. The most important thing is not to make a decision in a hurry.

- ² _____ a list of the positive and negative points for both options. Then decide which points are most important and ³ _____ the two lists.

- If you ⁴ _____ other people for their advice, don't ask more than one or two. If you ask a lot of people, this will probably ⁵ _____ you.

- ⁶ _____ your imagination to help you. Imagine yourself in both situations. How do you ⁷ _____? Relaxed or stressed?

- When you've made a decision, ⁸ _____ a bit before you tell other people, to see how you feel. If you feel comfortable with your decision after an hour, you have probably made the right decision.

- Finally, remember that you can't ⁹ _____ everything. Choosing one of two possibilities always means that you can't have the one you didn't choose. And it's impossible to *always* ¹⁰ _____ the right decision!

Adapted from a British newspaper

5 VOCABULARY noun formation

> ⚠ With some verbs you can make a noun by adding *-ion*, *-sion*, or *-ation*, for example, *decide > decision*; *imagine > imagination*

a Complete the chart.

Verb	Noun
confuse	confusion
decide	decision
imagine	imagination
inform	_____
elect	_____
invite	_____
organize	_____
educate	_____
translate	_____
communicate	_____

b **6.10** Listen and check. Underline the stressed syllable in the verbs and nouns.

1 How do you pronounce *-sion* and *-tion*?
2 Where is the stress in nouns which finish in *-ion*?

c Complete the questions with a noun from a.

1 When was the last time you had to make a big _____?
2 What kind of _____ do you often get from the Internet?
3 When was the last time you had an _____ to a wedding?
4 Which party won the last general _____ in your country?
5 Do you belong to any _____ (for example, *Greenpeace*, etc.)?
6 What do you think is the best form of _____, e-mail, phone, or text-message?

d In pairs, ask and answer the questions. Ask for more information.

6
D

G *should / shouldn't*
V *get*
P /ʊ/, sentence stress

You should talk to her.

What should I do?

1 LISTENING & READING

a Read this extract from a TV and radio guide.

1 What kind of programme is it?
2 Why do people call the programme?
3 Would you call a programme like this?

b **6.11** Listen to three people phoning *What's the Problem?* and complete the sentences with one word.

clothes	jealousy	money

Barbara's problem is about _____.
Kevin's problem is about _____.
Catherine's problem is about _____.

RADIO GUIDE

WHAT'S THE PROBLEM?
Weekdays 8.00–8.45p.m.

Daily advice programme with Julian Greenwood. Whatever your problem, call the programme and ask for help. Listeners can e-mail their suggestions to the *What's the problem?* website. Today's subject is 'friends'.

c Now listen again. What exactly are their problems? Compare what you understood with your partner.

d Read the e-mails which listeners sent to the *What's the problem?* website. Match two e-mails to each problem. Write Barbara, Kevin, or Catherine.

RADIO FM	MESSAGE BOARDS

AUTHOR	MESSAGE	AUTHOR	MESSAGE
1 Malcolm	Hi _____, I think you should talk to your girlfriend, not your friend. She might like the way your friend treats her. Perhaps that's why he does it. Why don't you tell her to ask him to stop? Malcolm	**4** Silvia	*Hi _____, I think it depends if your friend is good company or not. If he is then I think you should pay for him. If not, don't tell him where you're going when you go out.* Silvia
2 Maria	*Dear_____, If I were you, I wouldn't say anything to your friend. I think you should lock your clothes in a cupboard. She'll soon get the message, and that way you'll stay friends.* Maria	**5** Sandy	Dear_____, When your friend gets home tonight I think you should talk to her. Say 'I'm really sorry but I'm a bit obsessive about my things. I don't like other people touching them.' That way she'll stop but she won't get angry or offended. Sandy
3 Darren	Hi _____, You shouldn't be so sensitive. It's not really a problem, it just shows your friend thinks you have good taste. And don't argue with your friend. Women aren't worth it. Darren	**6** Martyn	Hi _____, You definitely shouldn't pay for him. When the waiter brings the bill, pretend that nobody has money to pay for him. Then he'll have to make an excuse to the waiter and maybe he'll learn that he has to pay for himself. Martyn

e Now read the e-mails again. In pairs, say which advice you think is best for each person and why.

2 GRAMMAR *should / shouldn't*

a Highlight examples of *should* and *shouldn't* in the e-mails on p.70.

b Does *You should talk to your girlfriend* mean…?
   1 You have to talk to your girlfriend.
   2 I think it's a good idea if you talk to your girlfriend.

c ⬤ **p.136 Grammar Bank 6D.** Read the rules and do the exercises.

3 PRONUNCIATION & SPEAKING /ʊ/

a (6.12) Listen and repeat. Write the words.
   1 /ʃʊd/   = *should*
   2 /ˈʃʊdnt/ =
   3 /wʊd/   =
   4 /ˈwʊdnt/ =
   5 /kʊd/   =
   6 /ˈkʊdnt/ =

b (6.13) Listen and repeat these sentences. Copy the rhythm.
   1 You should <u>talk</u> to your <u>friend</u>.
   2 You <u>shouldn't</u> be so <u>sensitive</u>.
   3 You should <u>lock</u> your <u>clothes</u> in a <u>cupboard</u>.
   4 You <u>definitely</u> <u>shouldn't</u> <u>pay</u> for your <u>friend</u>.
   5 <u>What</u> should I <u>do</u>?
   6 <u>Should</u> I <u>write</u> to him?

4 WRITING & SPEAKING

a Choose one of the problems and write a short note giving advice.

1	It's my girlfriend's birthday next week and I want to give her a surprise with a special present or a special evening somewhere. What should I do?
2	My friend has gone away on holiday for two weeks and I'm looking after her cat. Yesterday I couldn't find the cat anywhere. My friend is coming home in three days. I'm desperate. Should I phone her now and tell her? What should I do?
3	My best friend wants to borrow some money to help her buy a car. I have the money, and she says she'll pay me back next year. But I'm worried that it's not a good idea to lend money to friends. What should I do?
4	I really want to get fit and do more exercise. The problem is I hate going to gyms, and they're very expensive. And there are no parks near me to go running. What should I do?

b In pairs, read other student's notes. Decide which problem they refer to. Do you agree with the advice? Why (not)?

5 VOCABULARY *get*

a Look at these sentences from **1**. Match the examples of *get* with meanings A–D.
   1 I'm sure you'll soon **get** some e-mails with good advice. ☐
   2 When your friend **gets** home tonight you should talk to her. ☐
   3 She won't **get** angry with you. ☐
   4 I **get on** very **well** with her. ☐

   A receive   B be friendly with
   C become   D arrive

b ⬤ **p.152 Vocabulary Bank** *get*

c In pairs, do the **get** questionnaire.

1 Do you ever **get to** school / work late? When was the last time?

2 When was the last time you **got lost**? Where were you trying to go? What happened?

3 What makes you **get angry**? When was the last time you got really angry? Why?

4 When was the last time you **got a present**? What was it? Who was it from?

5 Who do you **get on with** best in your family? Is there anybody you don't get on with?

6 What do you think is the best age to **get married**? Why?

7 Which problems in your country are **getting better**? Which are **getting worse**?

ASKING FOR HELP

6.14 Listen and <u>underline</u> the right phrase.

1 Allie asks the receptionist for some **aspirin / painkillers**.
2 Allie has a **headache / backache**.
3 The receptionist **gives / doesn't give** her medicine.
4 Allie **wants / doesn't want** a doctor.
5 The pharmacy **is / isn't** near the hotel.

🇺🇸 US English	*pharmacy*
🇬🇧 UK English	*chemist's*

ASKING FOR MEDICINE

a **6.15** Cover the dialogue and listen. What does the pharmacist give her? How often does she have to take them? How much are they?

YOU HEAR	YOU SAY
Good morning. Can I help you?	I have a bad cold. Do you have something I can take?
What _____ do you have?	I have a headache and a cough.
Do you have a _____?	No, I don't think so.
Does your back _____?	No.
Are you allergic to any drugs?	I'm allergic to penicillin.
No problem. These are _____.	
These will make you feel _____.	How many do I have to take?
Two every four hours.	Sorry? How often?
Every four hours. If you don't feel better in _____ hours, you should see a doctor.	OK, thanks. How much are they?
$4.75, please.	Thank you.
You're welcome.	

b Listen again. Complete the **YOU HEAR** phrases.

aspirin	better	hurt	symptoms
temperature		twenty-four	

c **6.16** Listen and repeat the **YOU SAY** phrases. <u>Copy</u> the <u>rhythm</u>.

d In pairs, roleplay the dialogue. **A** (book open) you're the pharmacist, **B** (book closed) you're Allie. Swap roles.

SOCIAL ENGLISH   talking about the party

a **6.17** Listen and mark the sentences T (true) or F (false).

1 Mark apologizes for getting angry last night.
2 Allie thinks Brad is annoying.
3 Brad isn't Allie's type of man.
4 Today is Allie's last day.
5 They're going to have dinner on a boat.

USEFUL PHRASES

M B_____ you!
M I'm really sorry a_____ (last night).
A I don't m_____. You choose.
M H_____ about (a boat trip around the bay)?
A That s_____ fantastic.
A It's a p_____.

b Complete the **USEFUL PHRASES**. Listen again and check.

c **6.18** Listen and repeat the phrases. How do you say them in your language?

Study Link MultiROM

From: **Daniel**

To: Alessandra
Subject: Exams

Hi Alessandra!

Thanks for your last e-mail. I hope your exams went well. I have some exciting news and I'm writing to ¹ _ask_ for your advice.

I ² _____ to go on holiday to Argentina next year. What do you ³ _____ is the best month for me to come? I can only come for three weeks, so which places do you think I should ⁴ _____? Do you think I should ⁵ _____ a car or travel around by bus or train?

I'm planning to ⁶ _____ a few days in and around Mendoza, and it would be great if we could ⁷ _____. Can you ⁸ _____ a good hotel (not too expensive)?

Hope to hear from you soon!

Best wishes,
Daniel

a Read the e-mail and complete it with these verbs.

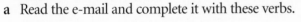

~~ask~~   hire   meet   recommend   spend   think   visit   want

b Imagine that Daniel has written to *you* about visiting *your* country. Plan how you're going to answer his questions. Compare with a partner.

c Look at the **USEFUL PHRASES**. What are the missing words?

USEFUL PHRASES

1 Thanks _____ your e-mail.
2 It was great to hear _____ you again.
3 I'm really happy that you want _____ visit my country.
4 I think you should come _____ July.
5 If I were you, I'd travel _____ bus.
6 I'm looking forward _____ seeing you soon.

WRITE an e-mail to Daniel. Use the phrases in **c** to help you.

Paragraph 1   Thank him for his e-mail, etc.
Paragraph 2   Answer his questions about your country. Give reasons.
Paragraph 3   Answer his question about your town. Give reasons.

CHECK your e-mail for mistakes (grammar , punctuation , and spelling).

6 What do you remember?

GRAMMAR

Circle the correct answer, a, b, or c.

What's _____ name?
a yours b your c you

1 If we start walking, the bus _____.
a come
b came
c will come

2 James _____ come to the party if his ex-girlfriend is there.
a won't
b don't
c doesn't

3 If we _____ queues, the other will move more quickly.
a change
b will change
c changed

4 What would you do if you _____ a bear?
a saw
b will see
c see

5 If we had a garden, we _____ a dog.
a 'll have
b 'd have
c had

6 I _____ go to the party. I'm not sure.
a might
b will
c may to

7 The petrol station _____ open today. It's a holiday.
a may not be
b may not to be
c may to

8 I think you _____ go to the doctor.
a would
b should to
c should

9 She _____ come home so late.
a not should
b shouldn't
c shouldn't to

10 If I _____ you, I'd talk to your girlfriend.
a were
b be
c am

10

VOCABULARY

a confusing verbs

Cross out the wrong verb.

I don't **watch** / ~~look at~~ TV very often.
1 Where did you **know** / **meet** your husband?
2 Shh! They're **making** / **doing** an exam.
3 How much money does he **earn** / **win**?
4 He was **carrying** / **wearing** a black umbrella.
5 You **look** / **look like** your sister. You have the same eyes.

b animals

Write the names of the animals.

It's a popular pet and it barks.   _dog_
1 It's a big cat and it lives in Africa.   _____
2 It has eight legs and it eats flies.   _____
3 People ride this animal in races.   _____
4 It's the largest animal in the sea.   _____
5 It's a male cow and it can be dangerous.   _____

c noun formation

Make nouns from these verbs.

imagine   _imagination_
1 communicate   _____
2 organize   _____
3 discuss   _____
4 translate   _____
5 decide   _____

15

PRONUNCIATION

a Underline the word with a different sound

1	rob	lose	borrow	problem
2	we'll	meet	lion	sheep
3	carry	camel	wasp	happen
4	ask	start	fall	shark
5	zoo	food	you'll	mouse

b Underline the stressed syllable.

infor<u>ma</u>tion

advice   crocodile   decision   happen   translation

10

74

CAN YOU UNDERSTAND THIS TEXT?

a Read the article and match the questions and answers.

A question of principles

The first of a new series in which celebrities answer questions on moral dilemmas. This week, radio presenter Stephen Bruce.

A ☐ If your girlfriend was allergic to the dog you've had for ten years, would you give your dog away?

B ☐ If your boss gave you tickets to the theatre and you forgot to go, would you tell him the truth when he asked?

C ☐ If your young daughter's hamster died, would you buy an identical one or tell her the truth?

D ☐ If a colleague at work told everyone that he was 45 but you knew he was five years older, would you keep his secret?

E ☐ If a celebrity was having a secret affair with your neighbour, would you sell the story to a newspaper?

1 I'd tell everybody the truth, probably in front of him. I think telling lies about your age is ridiculous.

2 No, I'd say that it was the best show I've ever seen! I wouldn't want to offend him. But he would probably guess I was lying.

3 I'm afraid the dog would win! I'd tell my girlfriend that my dog and I had been together for a long time but that she might not be here next week.

4 It would be an interesting story – my neighbour is a 92-year-old, bald Swedish man! No, I wouldn't. I'd just tell my partner.

5 I'd buy another one. It happened to me once when the children's goldfish died. I bought another one but they saw that it was different. I told them it had put on weight.

b Read the article again. Guess the meaning of the highlighted words or phrases. Check with the teacher or your dictionary.

CAN YOU UNDERSTAND THESE PEOPLE?

a **6.19** Listen and circle the correct answer, a, b, or c.

1 The man and woman decide to _____.
   a walk   b wait   c get a taxi
2 The woman _____ Deborah.
   a knows   b hasn't met   c wouldn't like to meet
3 Is the woman afraid of mice?
   a Yes   b No   c We don't know
4 Where does the man decide to go?
   a home   b to the pub   c to the cinema
5 What pet does the woman think he should buy?
   a a fish   b a cat   c a hamster

b **6.20** Listen and mark the sentences T (true) or F (false).

1 Dave got married five years ago.
2 His wife has just had a baby.
3 Dave's wife doesn't give him much attention.
4 Dave is more tired than his wife.
5 The advice he gets is to help his wife more.

CAN YOU SAY THIS IN ENGLISH?

a Can you…? Yes (✓)

☐ say three things you'll do if it rains tomorrow
☐ say what you would do if you were attacked by a crocodile
☐ say what you might do this weekend
☐ say what you should or shouldn't do if you have problems sleeping

b Write second conditional questions.

1 What / you do if / lose / wallet?
2 What / you do if / win the lottery?
3 What / you do if / find some money in the street?
4 What / you do if / have more free time?
5 What / you do if / can speak perfect English?

c Ask your partner the questions in **b**. Ask for more information.

7 A

G present perfect + *for* and *since*
V words related to fear
P /ɪ/ and /aɪ/, sentence stress

> I've been afraid of spiders since I was a child.

Famous fears and phobias

1 READING & VOCABULARY

a Match the words with the pictures.

flying ☐
heights ☐
closed spaces ☐
open spaces ☐
snakes ☐
spiders ☐
wasps ☐
water ☐

b Are you afraid of any of these things? Why? Do you know any people who are?

> I'm afraid of flying.

> I have a friend who is afraid of water. He can't swim.

c Read the article and complete each paragraph with a word from **a**.

d Underline the four words in the text related to being afraid.

2 GRAMMAR present perfect + *for* and *since*

a Read about Winona Ryder again and answer the questions.

When did she begin to be afraid of water?
In _____ .

Is she afraid of water now?   YES/NO

b Complete the answers with a year or a number of years.

How long has she been afraid of water?
She has been afraid of water **since** _____ .
She has been afraid of water **for** _____ years.

c Complete the rule with *for* and *since*.

Use _____ with a period of time.
Use _____ with a point in time.

d ➲ p.138 **Grammar Bank 7A.** Read the rules and do the exercises.

We're all afraid...

Famous people have phobias like the rest of us, and sometimes they seriously affect their lives.

Winona Ryder, American actress

Winona Ryder has been afraid of _____ since 1983. When she was 12 years old she fell into a lake and nearly died. Luckily someone pulled her out, and after a few minutes she came back to life again. It can be a real problem when she's making a film. For example, in some of the scenes in *Alien III*, she had to go in a boat and she was terrified.

Rupert Grint, British actor

Rupert Grint has been afraid of _____ since he was a child. In this respect he is like the character he played in the *Harry Potter* films, Ron Weasley, who is also frightened of them. Rupert had a very hard time in the second *Harry Potter* film where he and Harry had to fight a giant one (the size of an elephant) with very hairy legs!

Dennis Bergkamp, ex-international footballer

Dennis Bergkamp has been afraid of _____ since 1994. He was on a plane in the USA with the Dutch national team during the World Cup. A journalist said that there was a bomb on the plane (there wasn't), and everybody started to panic, including Dennis. He decided never to travel by plane again. Because of his fear Bergkamp could not play in many important matches for Holland, Inter Milan, and Arsenal.

3 LISTENING

a **7.1** Listen to Scott, a doctor talking about his cat phobia. What happens if he sees a cat?

b Listen again and answer the questions.

1 What's the medical name of his phobia?
2 How long has he had his phobia?
3 How did it start?

4 Does his phobia affect his work?
5 What treatment is he having?
6 Does he think his phobia will disappear?

4 PRONUNCIATION /ɪ/ and /aɪ/, sentence stress

a Put these words in the right column.

child   children   in   I've   like   life   line
live (v)   mine   minute   since   win

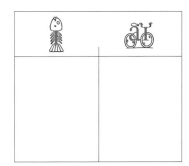

b **7.2** Listen and check. Practise saying the words.

c Practise saying the sentences.

I've lived here since I was a child.
I've liked wine since I lived in Italy.

d **7.3** Listen and repeat the questions. Copy the rhythm.

1 lived here	have you lived here	How long have you lived here?
2 known him	have you known him	How long have you known him?
3 been married	have they been married	How long have they been married?
4 had his dog	has he had his dog	How long has he had his dog?

5 SPEAKING

Ask and answer in pairs.

A ask **B** six *How long …?* questions with a verb phrase.

B answer with *for* or *since*.
Give more information if you can.
Then swap roles.

How long have you known your oldest friend?

Since we were at primary school together.

know → the other students in this class
know → your oldest friend
know → the teacher

live → in this town
live → in your house or flat

be → in this school
be → married
be → a lawyer, nurse, etc.

have → your car
have → the shoes you're wearing
have → your watch

7

B Born to direct

G present perfect or past simple?
V biographies
P word stress

> He was born in Knoxville, Tennessee.

1 VOCABULARY & PRONUNCIATION

a Under<u>line</u> the stressed syllable in the highlighted words below.

Events in your life

go to university	☐	fall in love	☐
be born	☐	get divorced	☐
go to primary school	☐	have children	☐
start work	☐	get married	☐
leave school	☐	go to secondary school	☐
die	☐	separate	☐
retire	☐		

b **7.4** Listen and check. Practise saying the phrases.

c Number the expressions in what you think is a logical order. Compare with a partner. Do you agree?

2 READING & SPEAKING

a Look at the film photos. In pairs, answer the questions.

1 Who directed the films?
2 Have you seen either of the films? What kind of films are they?

b Read fifteen facts about the lives of the two directors. In pairs, decide which eight are about Hitchcock, and which seven are about Tarantino. Write **H** or **T**.

c **A** re-read the facts about Hitchcock, and **B** about Tarantino.

d Work in pairs.

A (Book closed) in your own words say everything you can remember about Hitchcock.
B (Book open) listen and help. Then swap roles. **B** Say everything you can remember about Tarantino.

3 GRAMMAR present perfect or past simple?

a Answer the questions.

1 Look at the eight facts about Hitchcock's life. What tense are all the verbs? Why?
2 Look at the seven facts about Tarantino's life. What three tenses are there? Why?

b ⟳ **p.138 Grammar Bank 7B.** Read the rules and do the exercises.

Hitchcock or Tarantino?

1 He appeared in small roles in almost all of his films. **H**

2 He was a very intelligent child, but he had difficulties with reading and writing. He left school when he was 15 and went to work in a cinema, where he checked tickets at the entrance. ☐

3 He was born in London in 1899. ☐

4 His muse is Uma Thurman, who he has directed in several of his most successful films. ☐

The Birds

5 He was married and his daughter Patricia appeared in several of his films. ☐

6 He went to school at St. Ignatius College, in London, and later studied art at the University of London. ☐

7 He was famous for not liking actors. He once said 'all actors are children and should be treated like cattle.' ☐

8 He was born in Knoxville, Tennesee in 1963. ☐

Kill Bill

Alfred Hitchcock

9 He spent a short time in prison because he could not pay a parking ticket. ☐

10 His muse was Grace Kelly (later Princess Grace of Monaco), who he directed in several of his most successful films. ☐

11 He died in 1980. ☐

12 He began his career as an actor. His biggest role was in an episode of the TV series *The Golden Girls*. He played the part of a man who impersonated Elvis Presley. ☐

Quentin Tarantino

13 He never won an Oscar for Best Director, although he was nominated five times. When the Academy finally gave him an honorary Oscar he received a standing ovation. He just said, 'Thank you' and left the stage. ☐

14 He has been nominated for an Oscar for Best Director but he hasn't won one yet. ☐

15 He says he hates drugs and violence but they appear a lot in his films. ☐

4 SPEAKING

a Think about a member of your family (who is alive), for example a parent, uncle, aunt, or grandparent. Prepare to answer the questions below about their life.

The past
Where / born?
Where / go to school?
What / do after (he/she) left school?
When / start work?
When / get married?

The present
Where / live now?
  How long / live there?
Is he / she married?
  How long / be married?
Is he / she retired?
  How long has he / she be retired?
How many children / have?

b A interview B about their person. Ask for more information. Then swap roles.

5 LISTENING

a Look at the photo of Sofia Coppola and her father. What do they both do?

b You're going to listen to part of a TV programme about Sofia Coppola. Look at the information below. Before you listen guess what the connection is with her.

Francis Ford Coppola   Sofia Coppola

> I think she directed *The Godfather*.

> No, she was too young.

1 New York 1971

7 *Lost in Translation* (Oscar nomination)

2 *The Godfather*

6 Spike Jonze (film director)

3 *The Godfather Part III* (Mary Corleone)

5 1999 – *The Virgin Suicides*

4 California Institute of Art

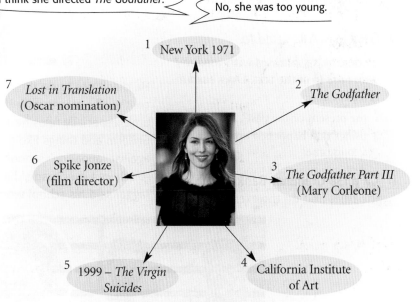

c 7.5 Now listen and make notes. Compare with a partner.

d In pairs, ask and answer the questions.

Have you seen any of the films in **b**? Which one(s)? Did you like them?
Have you seen a good film recently? Which one? Who was in it?
What's the best film you've seen this year? Who directed it?
What's the worst film you've seen this year? Who directed it?

7C

G used to
V school subjects: *history, geography*, etc.
P sentence stress: *used to / didn't use to*

> Did you use to like primary school?
> Yes, I did.

I used to be a rebel

1 READING

a Look at the picture. Does it make you think of your school? Why (not)?

b Look at the photos and read the article about Mick Jagger. Do you think he was *really* a rebel when he was at school? Why (not)?

c Read the text again. In pairs, guess the meaning of the highlighted words.

2 GRAMMAR *used to*

a Underline six phrases with *used to / didn't use to* in the text. Does *used to* refer to…

1 the present or the past?
2 things that happened once or for a long time?

b ⭘ **p.138 Grammar Bank 7C.** Read the rules and do the exercises.

A famous rebel – but was he really?

MICK JAGGER went back to his old school recently – for the first time since he left in 1961. He was invited to the school to open the 'Mick Jagger Performing Arts centre', a new music and drama department at Dartford Grammar School.

Jagger said that he was 'honoured' that the centre was named after him. But in a newspaper interview two days before he told a journalist that in fact he hated school and that he used to be a rebel.

He didn't use to do the homework – 'there was far too much'– and he was continually at war with the teachers. He used to break the rules all the time, especially rules he thought were stupid, about how to wear the school uniform and things like that. Once he even organized a mass protest against 'appalling' school dinners. 'It was probably the greatest contribution to school I ever made,' he said. Although he made a good start at school, Jagger said his school work deteriorated because of 'music and girls'.

Mick Jagger in his school basketball team

However, according to one of his old school friends, musician Dick Taylor, this is not true. He says that Mick didn't use to be a rebel at all – he was quite bright and used to work hard. He also used to do a lot of sport.

When Mick Jagger left school, he had seven O-levels and two A-levels, which at that time were good qualifications – so perhaps Dick's memory is better than Mick's…

Adapted from a British newspaper

3 LISTENING

a Look at the photos of Melissa when she was at school and today. How has she changed?

b 🔊 **7.6** Listen to her talking about her school days. Was she a rebel or a 'good girl' at school? What does she do now?

c Listen again. Mark the sentences T (true) or F (false).

1 Melissa is a teenager in the photo.
2 She used to write things on the walls.
3 She didn't like any of the subjects at school.
4 Her least favourite subject was PE.
5 The PE teacher made them try to do difficult things.
6 She used to break the rules about the school uniform.
7 She wanted to be a doctor.
8 Her parents wanted her to be a teacher.

4 PRONUNCIATION sentence stress

> ⚠️ *used to* and (*didn't*) *use to* are both pronounced /juːstə/.

a 🔊 **7.7** Listen and underline the stressed words. Then listen and repeat.

1 I used to go out a lot.
2 He used to hate school.
3 They didn't use to be friends.
4 She didn't use to like him.
5 Did you use to wear glasses?

b 🔊 **7.8** Now listen and write six more sentences.

5 VOCABULARY school subjects

a Match the words with the pictures.

PE (=physical education) ☐
geography ☐
technology ☐
maths ☐
history ☐
foreign languages (English, etc.) ☐
literature ☐
science (physics, chemistry, and biology) ☐

b 🔊 **7.9** Listen and practise saying the words.

c Think about when you were 11 or 12 years old. Talk about each subject with one of the expressions below. Say why.

I used / didn't use to like _____.

> I didn't use to like maths. I was really bad at it.

6 SPEAKING

a Think about when you were 11 or 12. Were these things true or false about you? Why?

I used to be a rebel.	I used to do a lot of sport.
I used to work hard.	I used to wear glasses.
I used to like all the teachers.	I used to wear a uniform.
I used to hate school.	I used to have longer hair.

b Work in groups of three.

A tell **B** and **C** about how you used to be. **B** and **C** listen and ask for more information. Then swap roles. Did you have anything in common?

> I didn't use to be a rebel. I was a good boy.

7 🔊 **7.10** SONG ♫ *It's all over now*

7
D

G passive
V verbs: *invent, discover*, etc.
P *-ed*, sentence stress

It was invented by a woman.

The mothers of invention

the dishwasher

disposable nappies

nylon stockings

the vacuum cleaner

the bullet-proof vest

Tipp-Ex

1 LISTENING

a Look at the photos. Five of these things were invented by women. In pairs, decide which five you think they are.

b **7.11** Now listen to a radio programme about inventions. Were you right? Complete the sentences with the invention.

1 _____ was invented by Josephine Cochrane in 1886.
2 _____ were invented by Mary Anderson in 1903.
3 _____ were invented by Marion Donovan in 1950.
4 _____ was invented by Bette Nesmith Graham in 1956.
5 _____ was invented by Stephanie Kwolek in 1966.

c Listen again and answer the questions.

1 What happened after Josephine Cochrane's dinner parties?
2 What was the problem with cars in 1903 when it rained or snowed?
3 How many disposable nappies are used every day?
4 What was Bette Nesmith Graham's job?
5 What was special about the material Stephanie Kwolek invented?

d Which of the five inventions do you think was the best?

2 GRAMMAR passive

a Make five true sentences using the words in the chart.

The dishwasher	is called	Tipp-Ex today.
Disposable nappies	was invented	by Marion Donovan.
More than 55 million nappies	are protected	every day.
Mrs Graham's invention	were invented	by the bullet-proof vest.
Policemen all over the world	are used	by an American woman.

The dishwasher was invented by an American woman.

b Look at these two sentences and answer the questions.

a An American woman invented the dishwasher.
b The dishwasher was invented by an American woman.

1 Do the sentences have the same meaning?
2 Do the sentences have the same emphasis?
3 Which sentence is in the passive?

c ⭕ **p.138 Grammar Bank 7D.** Read the rules and do the exercises.

windscreen wipers

the Biro

the washing machine

3 READING & VOCABULARY

a Complete the text below with the correct verb in the right form.

base	create	design (x2)	discover	~~invent~~	name	use	write

Did you know...?

Text-messaging was ¹_invented_ by the Finnish company Nokia. They wanted to help Finnish teenagers, who were very shy. They found it easier to text their friends than to phone them.

The first bikini was ²_____ by two Frenchmen. It was ³_____ after Bikini Atoll, the island where the atomic bomb was first tested. The Frenchmen thought that the bikini would have a similar effect on men as a bomb exploding.

Light bulbs are ⁴_____ specially to last only a certain number of hours. It would be possible to make light bulbs that lasted forever, but then the manufacturers wouldn't make so much money.

The first Harry Potter book was ⁵_____ in a café in Edinburgh. JK Rowling was unemployed, and she didn't have enough money to pay for heating, so she wrote it in the café where it was warmer.

Although penicillin was ⁶_____ by Alexander Fleming, he didn't know how to make it into a medicine. It was first made into a medicine ten years later, by an Australian scientist Howard Florey.

Spiders were ⁷_____ as a cure for toothache in the 17th century. They were first made into a paste, and then put on the bad tooth.

Sherlock Holmes, the great detective was ⁸_____ by writer Arthur Conan Doyle. Holmes was ⁹_____ on a real person – Doyle's teacher at medical school, who was famous for saying to his students, 'What can you tell me by just observing the patient?'

b Read the facts again. In pairs, say which one is the most surprising.

4 PRONUNCIATION   *-ed*, sentence stress

a How is the *–ed* pronounced in these past participles? Put them in the right column.

based	designed	directed	discovered	invented
named	painted	produced	used	

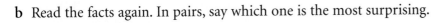 /d/	/t/	/ɪd/

b **7.12** Listen and check. Underline the stressed syllable in each multi-syllable verb.

c **7.13** Listen and repeat the sentences. Copy the rhythm. Which words are stressed?

1 The film was based on a true story.
2 These clothes were designed by Armani.
3 This wine is produced near here.
4 My sister was named after our grandmother.
5 These pictures were painted by my aunt.
6 Garlic is used a lot in French cooking.

5 SPEAKING

❯ **Communication** *Passives quiz A p.111 B p.115.* Make sentences for your partner to decide if they are true or false.

7 A boat trip

PRACTICAL ENGLISH

HOW TO GET THERE

7.14 Listen to Mark and Allie and mark the sentences T (true) or F (false).

1 Allie's feeling worse.
2 Mark thinks Allie might get cold.
3 They're going to get a taxi to the bay.
4 Allie wants to be at the hotel again at 1.00 p.m.
5 She's expecting an important visitor.

BUYING TICKETS

a **7.15** Cover the dialogue and listen. Complete the sentences.

The next boat leaves at ___ a.m. The trip takes ___ hour(s) and costs ___.

〈 YOU SAY	YOU HEAR
Good morning.	Good morning, sir.
What time does the next boat leave?	At 10.00.
How long does it take?	_____ an hour.
Where exactly does the boat go?	It goes _____ the bridge, _____ Angel Island and _____ Alcatraz, and then _____ here.
Can we get anything to eat or drink on the boat?	Yes, ma'am, there's a _____ bar.
Can I have two tickets, please?	Sure. Two _____.
How much is that?	That's $40.
Here you are.	Thank you, sir.
Thank you.	

b Listen again and complete the YOU HEAR phrases.

c **7.16** Listen and repeat the YOU SAY phrases. Copy the rhythm.

d In pairs, roleplay the dialogue. **A** (book open) you're the ticket seller, **B** (book closed) you're Mark and Allie. Swap roles.

SOCIAL ENGLISH on the boat

a **7.17** Listen and answer the questions.

1 Does Allie prefer San Francisco to London?
2 Does she think she could live there? Why (not)?
3 What did the building on Alcatraz use to be?
4 What's the weather like?
5 What does Mark ask the boatman to do?

USEFUL PHRASES

M What do you t_____ of (San Francisco)?
A Why do you a_____?
M Oh, no reason. I j_____ wondered.
A I'm really l_____ forward to it.
M C_____ you take a photo of us, please?
B Are you r_____?

b Complete the USEFUL PHRASES. Listen again and check.

c **7.18** Listen and repeat the phrases. How do you say them in your language?

Study Link MultiROM

a Read the description and complete it with words from the box.

~~cathedral~~ completed designed roof steps statue view windows

b Match the questions with paragraphs 1–6.

Is there a view from the building? ☐
Describe the building outside. ☐
Describe the building inside. ☐
How much does it cost to go in? ☐
What's the most beautiful building in your town? Where is it? ☐
Who was it designed by? When was it built? ☐

c Find one spelling mistake in each paragraph and correct it.

> **WRITE** a description of a building in your town.
> Answer the questions in **b** in the right order.
>
> **CHECK** your description for mistakes (grammar ,
> punctuation , and spelling).

1 The most bea/tiful building in my town is
the ¹*cathedral* (the Duomo). It is in the
centre of Milan, in the Piazza del Duomo.

2 Nobody knows who it was ²_____ by,
but peopel think it was an architect from
northern Europe. Construction began in
1386, but the building wasn't ³_____
for another 500 years.

3 It is one of the largest cathedrals in the
world and it has 135 spires and 3,400
statues. On top of the Duomo there is
a gold ⁴_____ of the Madonna which
watches over the city. The statue is
called the 'Madonnina', or the little
Madonna, althought it is four metres tall.

4 Inside the Duomo it is quite dark. There
are beautiful big ⁵_____, and a lot of
intresting statues and monuments. In the
chapel of St Fina there are some
wonderful frescoes by Ghirlandaio.

5 One of the best things you can do in Milan
is to go up to the ⁶_____ of the Duomo.
The ⁷_____ is fantastic – on a cleer day
you can see the Italian Alps. You can get
the lift, or if you are feeling energetic you
can walk up the 250 ⁸_____.

6 It is free to go in, but you must
dress apropriately.

85

GRAMMAR

Circle the correct answer, a, b, or c.

What's _____ name?

a yours   (b) your   c you

1 I _____ in this house since I was a child.
   a live
   b 'm living
   c 've lived

2 My father's had his car _____.
   a for two years
   b since two years
   c two years ago

3 How long _____ afraid of flying?
   a are you
   b have you been
   c you have been

4 Tom Cruise and Nicole Kidman _____ married for ten years, but divorced in 2001.
   a are
   b have been
   c were

5 When _____?
   a did Alfred Hitchcock die
   b is Alfred Hitchcock dead
   c has Alfred Hitchcock died

6 My brother _____ glasses.
   a used to wear
   b use to wear
   c used to wearing

7 I _____ like vegetables when I was a child.
   a don't use to
   b didn't use to
   c didn't used to

8 Radium _____ discovered by Pierre and Marie Curie.
   a is
   b were
   c was

9 *The Lord of the Rings* _____ by J.R.R. Tolkien.
   a wrote
   b was wrote
   c was written

10 Paper _____ the Chinese.
   a was invented by
   b invented for
   c was invented for | **10** |

VOCABULARY

a time expressions

Complete the sentences with *for* or *since*.

I've lived here ___since___ 1998.

1 I've had this pen _____ I was a child.
2 He's been married _____ last June.
3 They've known each other _____ a long time.
4 She's studied French literature _____ three years.
5 You've worn that sweater every day _____ Christmas!

b verb phrases

Complete the phrases with a verb.

| be | get | fall | ~~have~~ | leave | retire |

   ___have___ children
1 _____ in love
2 _____ school / university
3 _____ married / divorced
4 _____ when you're 65
5 _____ born

c school subjects

Complete the sentences with a school subject.

If you study *technology* you learn to use computers.

1 If you study _____ you learn about what happened in the past.
2 If you study _____ you learn about countries, mountains, rivers, etc.
3 If you study _____ you learn to add, multiply, etc.
4 If you study _____ you learn physics and chemistry.
5 If you study _____ you learn about plants and animals. | **15** |

PRONUNCIATION

a Underline the word with a different sound.

1	since	time	child	life
2	school	food	cartoon	book
3	use	ugly	university	uniform
4	scene	science	scarf	since
5	change	teacher	school	children

b Underline the stressed syllable.

infor**ma**tion

afraid   favourite   directed   discovered   invented | **10** |

What can you do?

CAN YOU UNDERSTAND THIS TEXT?

a Read the article quickly. What is surprising about Lady Morton?

The world's most experienced driver?

One of Scotland's most active ¹ centenarians , Lady Morton, has been a driver for nearly 80 years, although she has never taken a driving test. But last week she had her first ever accident – she hit a traffic island when she took her new car for a drive in Edinburgh.

Lady Morton, who celebrated her 100th birthday in July, ² was given the Nissan Micra as a surprise present. Yesterday she talked about the accident. 'I wasn't going fast, but I hit a traffic island. I couldn't see it, because it had no lights, which I think is ³ ridiculous . But I am all right and luckily my car wasn't badly ⁴ damaged .'

⁵ In spite of the accident , she is not planning to stop driving. 'Some people are just born to drive, and I think I am one of them. I've never taken a test, but I've been a good driver since the first time I got in a car. I'm musical, so I listen to the sound of the car to know when to change gear. Some people are very rude – they ask me if I'm still driving at my age. ⁶ It really annoys me .'

Lady Morton bought her first car in 1927. The ⁷ main change she has noticed since then is the traffic. 'It's ⁸ appalling . I don't mind it, because I am experienced, but I feel very sorry for beginners.'

Adapted from a British newspaper

b Tick (✓) the things the article says.
  1 Lady Morton has had a lot of accidents.
  2 She bought a Nissan Micra recently.
  3 She couldn't see the traffic island because she didn't have her lights on.
  4 She wasn't badly hurt.
  5 After her latest accident she needs a new car.
  6 She thinks she's a safe driver.
  7 The amount of traffic isn't a problem for her.

c Read the article again. Guess the meaning of the highlighted words or phrases. Check with the teacher or your dictionary.

CAN YOU UNDERSTAND THESE PEOPLE?

a **7.19** Listen. Circle a, b, or c.
  1 How long has Matt lived in Glasgow?
    a Since he was at university. b For six months. c For two years.
  2 John's sister _____ married.
    a is b is going to get c was
  3 He started running _____.
    a a few years ago b at school c a few days ago
  4 What's her favourite subject?
    a Geography b Literature c Maths
  5 When was the White Tower completed?
    a In the 17th century. b In 1068. c In 1285.

b **7.20** Listen and complete the table with a number or one word.

Ground floor:	¹ a collection of _____ by Graham Richmond.
First floor:	² children's _____
Entrance hall:	³ the museum _____
Price of guidebook:	⁴ _____
Museum closes at:	⁵ _____

CAN YOU SAY THIS IN ENGLISH?

a Can you...? Yes (✓)
  ☐ say how long you have lived in your town, worked in your job, etc.
  ☐ talk about the life of an old person in your family
  ☐ say three things you used to do when you were at (primary) school
  ☐ describe a famous building in your town

b Complete the questions with an auxiliary verb.
  1 How long _____ you been in this class?
  2 Where _____ your grandparents born?
  3 What TV programmes _____ you use to watch when you were a child?
  4 What's the oldest building in your town? When _____ it built?

c Ask your partner the questions in **b**. Ask for more information.

8
A

G something, anything, nothing, etc.
V adjectives ending -ed and -ing
P /e/, /əʊ/, /ʌ/

I didn't do anything at the weekend.

I hate weekends!

Most people say that Saturdays or Sundays are their favourite days of the week – but not everybody. For some people weekends are not much fun...

Marco from Brazil is a _____

'I hate the weekend. The weekend is when I'm busiest. I never go ¹ **any**_where_ and I don't really do ² **any**_____ except work. On Friday and Saturday nights we're usually full, and I have to be on my feet for seven or eight hours both days. We're supposed to close at 1.00, but people often don't leave until 1.30 or even later – they never think that we might want to go home. Luckily we close after lunch on Sunday, but when I get home, usually at about 5.30, I'm so tired that I don't want to see ³ **any**_____ or do ⁴ **any**_____ except lie on the sofa and watch TV. The best day of the week for me is Wednesday – that's my day off.'

Kirsten from Germany is a _____

'I must admit that for me now the weekends are more tiring than the week. During the week I have ⁵ **some**_____ to help me, but at the weekends we're on our own. My husband's always exhausted from his job and wants to relax, but ⁶ **no**_____ can relax with two small kids around. Our flat isn't very big so there's ⁷ **no**_____ you can go to have some peace and quiet. Before we had children I used to work too and weekends were perfect. We had ⁸ **no**_____ to do except enjoy ourselves. Now I'm really happy when it's Monday morning.'

Steve from the UK is a _____

'My weekend is usually quite stressful, more stressful than during the week. If we're playing at home I can't go out on Friday night. All my friends know that, so ⁹ **no**_____ invites me out on a Friday. I have ¹⁰ **some**_____ light to eat, and watch TV, and go to bed early. Very boring! On Saturday morning I usually relax and prepare myself mentally, as our home matches are usually at 3.00 in the afternoon. What I do on Saturday night depends on whether we win or lose. If we win, I have to go out with the team to celebrate. If we lose, we're too depressed to go ¹¹ **any**_____. When we play away, the weekend doesn't exist. We travel ¹² **some**_____, play, and then travel back again. I look forward to having a weekend just for me.'

1 READING

a Is the weekend your favourite part of the week? Why (not)?

b Read the article. In pairs, guess what the three people do.

c (8.1) Listen and check.

d Complete the sentences with **Marco**, **Kirsten**, or **Steve**.

1 _____ always gets home late on Saturdays.
2 _____ goes to bed early on Friday night.
3 _____ usually spends the weekend with the family.
4 _____ sometimes goes out on Saturday night.
5 _____ used to love the weekend.
6 _____ prefers Wednesdays to Saturdays.

e Read the texts again. Complete the words 1–12 with **-thing**, **-body**, or **-where**.

2 GRAMMAR *something, anything, nothing, etc.*

a Look again at 1–12 in the text. Complete the rules with *things*, *places*, and *people*.

Use *something*, *anything*, and *nothing* for _____.

Use *somebody*, *anybody*, and *nobody* for _____.

Use *somewhere*, *anywhere*, and *nowhere* for _____.

b ○ **p.140 Grammar Bank 8A.** Read the rules and do the exercises.

3 PRONUNCIATION /e/, /əʊ/, /ʌ/

a What are sounds 1–3?

1   2   3

b What sound do the pink letters make in each sentence? Write 1, 2, or 3.

1 Nobody knows where he goes. ☐
2 Somebody's coming to lunch. ☐
3 I never said anything. ☐
4 I've done nothing since Sunday. ☐
5 Don't tell anybody about the message. ☐
6 There's nowhere to go except home. ☐

c **8.2** Listen and check your answers. Practise saying the sentences.

4 VOCABULARY adjectives ending *-ed* and *-ing*

a Look at the two sentences from the article. What's the difference between *tired* and *tiring*?

I'm so **tired** that I don't want to see anybody.

Weekends are more **tiring** than week days.

b Look at the adjectives in **bold** in these sentences. How do you pronounce them?

1 Friday night is **bored** / **boring**. I never go out.
2 I'm **bored** / **boring** with my job. It's always the same.
3 If we lose we feel **depressed** / **depressing**.
4 My team never win. It's **depressed** / **depressing**.
5 Reading is very **relaxed** / **relaxing**.
6 I feel very **relaxed** / **relaxing** at the weekend.
7 His latest film is really **interesting** / **interested**.
8 I'm not very **interesting** / **interested** in sport.
9 I'm very **excited** / **exciting** about my holiday.
10 It was a really **excited** / **exciting** match.

c Cross out the wrong word.

5 SPEAKING

Ask and answer with a partner. Ask for more information too.

Every weekend

/ you normally have to work or study at weekends?
/ there anything you always watch on TV?
/ you normally have to buy anything on Saturdays?
/ have to do anything in the house (clean, etc.)?

Last weekend

/ you go anywhere exciting on Friday night?
/ do anything tiring on Saturday morning?
/ you meet anybody on Saturday night?
/ you do anything relaxing on Sunday?

Next weekend

/ you go away anywhere?
/ you do anything special on Saturday?
/ you go anywhere interesting on Sunday?

6 LISTENING

a **8.3** Listen and number the pictures 1–8.

b In pairs, use the pictures 1–8 to re-tell the story.

8 B

G quantifiers, *too, not enough*
V health and lifestyle
P /ʌ/, /uː/, /aɪ/, /e/; linking

How old is your body?

> I eat too much meat.
> I don't drink enough water.

How old are you? How old is your body? The answer to these two questions isn't always the same. Our body age can be much younger or much older than our calendar age (even eighteen years different!). We can now calculate our body age by answering questions about the way we live. If our body age is older than our calendar age, we should change our lifestyle.

EXERCISE
I know I'm too fat because I don't do enough exercise. I spend too much time sitting in studios. All I do is play squash, but I don't play very often – about once a month. I would go to a gym if I had more time.

DIET
I eat quite a lot of fresh food and a lot of fruit, but I probably eat too much meat. My girlfriend says I don't drink enough water. I drink a little alcohol – just a glass of red wine with my dinner. But I don't drink any beer. I drink a lot of coffee. It goes with the job.

LIFESTYLE
Like everybody I'm too busy! There aren't enough hours in the day. I love my job but I work too much (sometimes I spend 14 hours a day in the studio – that's too many). I often feel a bit tense and irritable. I smoke a few cigarettes when I go out, but I'm not a regular smoker. I only wear sunscreen when I go to the beach. My skin is quite dark so I don't think it's a problem.

PERSONALITY
I'm quite pessimistic. I always think that things will go wrong – and they usually do, especially at work.

SOCIAL LIFE
I don't have much free time but I have a few close friends and I try to see them regularly. If I'm too busy then I phone them.

DOCTOR'S VERDICT:
Tariq should do more exercise, for example he could walk to work. This would help him to control his stress. His diet is quite healthy but he should drink more water and less coffee. He must give up smoking. Although his skin is quite dark he should wear sunscreen all year round, even in winter. And he should try to be more positive.

Tariq, a record producer
Calendar age 32   Body age [   ]

1 READING

a Read the introduction to the article and answer the questions.

1 Is our body age the same as our calendar age?
2 How can we calculate our body age?
3 What should we do if our body age is older than our calendar age?

b Look at the photo of Tariq and read about him. <u>Underline</u> the things he does that are good. Circle the things he does that are bad. Compare with a partner.

c Cover the *Doctor's verdict*. What do you think he should do?

d Now read the *Doctor's verdict*. Was the advice the same as yours? What do you think his body age is?

2 GRAMMAR   quantifiers, *too, not enough*

a Can you remember how to use *much, many*, etc.? In pairs, choose the correct word or phrase for each sentence. Say why the other one is wrong.

1 How **much** / **many** coffee do you drink?
2 I don't eat **much** / **many** vegetables.
3 I eat **a lot of** / **many** bread.
4 I smoke **a lot** / **a lot of**.
5 **A** How much tea do you drink?
  B **Any** / **None**. I don't like it.

b Match the phrases 1–6 with the meanings A–F.

1 ☐ I drink **too much** coffee.   A I don't drink much.
2 ☐ I'm **too** fat.   B I need to do more.
3 ☐ I work **too many** hours.   C I have two or three.
4 ☐ I don't do **enough** exercise.   D I work more than I want.
5 ☐ I drink **a little** alcohol.   E I should be a bit thinner.
6 ☐ I have **a few** close friends.   F I drink more than I should.

c ➲ p.140 Grammar Bank 8B. Read the rules and do the exercises.

3 PRONUNCIATION /ʌ/, /uː/, /aɪ/, /e/; linking

a Cross out the word with a different pronunciation.

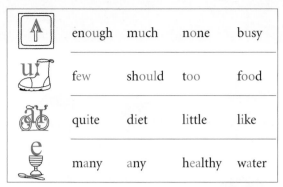

↑	enough	much	none	busy
👢	few	should	too	food
🚲	quite	diet	little	like
🥚	many	any	healthy	water

b **8.4** Listen and check. Practise saying the words.

> ⚠ Remember! When people speak quickly they don't separate the words.

c **8.5** Listen and write the six sentences.

d Listen and repeat the sentences. Copy the rhythm.

4 SPEAKING

a Read the questionnaire and circle your answers.

b Interview your partner and <u>underline</u> his / her answers. Ask for more information.

How much sport or exercise do you do? — A lot.

What do you do? — I go to the gym three times a week.

c ➲ **Communication** *Body age p.111.* Work out your body age.

d Look at your partner's answers. Give him / her some good advice.

I think you should do more exercise. For example…

What's your body age?
Do our quiz and find out

EXERCISE

1 How much do you walk a day?
a a lot   b quite a lot   c not much   d very little

2 How much sport and exercise do you do a week?
a a lot   b quite a lot   c a little   d none

DIET

3 How much fast food (processed and pre-prepared) do you eat?
a I eat too much.   b I eat quite a lot.
c I don't eat much.   d I don't eat any.

4 How many portions of fruit and vegetables do you eat per day?
a only a few   b quite a lot   c a lot

5 How much water do you drink?
a a lot   b quite a lot   c a little

6 What's your worst diet habit?
a I eat too much fat.   b I eat (or drink) too many sweet things.
c I eat (or drink) too much.   d none of these

LIFESTYLE

7 How many cigarettes do you smoke a day?
a none   b a few   c a lot

8 How would you describe yourself mentally?
a I am a very positive person.   b I am not positive enough.
c I'm quite pessimistic.

9 How would you describe your stress level?
a I am too stressed.   b I am stressed, but it's under control.
c I am quite relaxed.

10 How often do you wear sunscreen?
a all year   b only when I'm on holiday   c when it's sunny

SOCIAL LIFE

11 How many close friends do you see regularly?
a a lot   b quite a lot   c a few   d not many / none

12 How much time do you have for yourself?
a none   b not enough   c quite a lot

8C
G word order of phrasal verbs
V phrasal verbs
P /g/ and /dʒ/

I wake up and I turn on the radio.

Waking up is hard to do

1 VOCABULARY phrasal verbs

a Match the questions 1–7 with the pictures A–G.

1 What time do you **wake up** in the morning? ☐ *D*
2 Do you use an alarm clock to **wake up**? ☐
3 Do you **turn off** the alarm clock immediately? ☐
4 What's the first thing you **turn on** after you **wake up**? ☐
5 Do you **get up** immediately after you **wake up**? ☐
6 How do you feel when you first **get up**? ☐
7 When you get dressed, what's the last thing you **put on**? ☐

b Cover the questions and look at the pictures. Try to remember the questions.

c In pairs, use the pictures to ask and answer the questions.

d ➡ **p.153 Vocabulary Bank** *Phrasal verbs*.

2 GRAMMAR word order of phrasal verbs

a Look at the pictures 1–3 and <u>underline</u> the object of the phrasal verb in each sentence.

b Complete the rules about separable phrasal verbs with *noun* or *pronoun*.

  1 If the object of a phrasal verb is a _____, you can put it **after** the verb +*up*, *on*, etc.
    OR **between** the verb and *up*, *on*, etc.
  2 If the object of a phrasal verb is a _____, you **must** put it **between** the verb and *up*, *on*, etc.

c ➡ **p.140 Grammar Bank 8C.** Read the rules and do the exercises.

d Match the sentences. Then cover the sentences on the right. Try to remember them.

  1 Your mobile's ringing. *E* A You need to give it up.
  2 This is an important rule. ☐ B Put them away.
  3 I can't hear the music. ☐ C Turn it up.
  4 If you don't know what the words mean, ☐ D Throw it away.
  5 This is an immigration form. ☐ E ~~Turn it off.~~
  6 Coffee is bad for you. ☐ F Please fill it in.
  7 Your clothes are on the floor. ☐ G Write it down.
  8 That's rubbish. ☐ H look them up.

Turn off the alarm clock! 1

Turn the alarm clock off! 2

TURN IT OFF! 3

3 READING

a Do you know what these scientific words and expressions mean?

a gene   DNA   your 'body clock'   research

b Read the article about morning and evening people. Choose **a**, **b**, or **c**.

1 Scientists say that if we are bad at getting up in the morning, this is because
   a we are born like that.
   b we go to bed too late.
   c we drink too much coffee.

2 Researchers asked people questions about
   a the way they lived.
   b science.
   c sport and exercise.

3 They discovered that people who have a short 'clock' gene
   a are better in the morning than in the evening.
   b get tired very early.
   c are better in the evening than in the morning.

4 They recommend that people who have a long 'clock' gene
   a should only work in the afternoon and evening.
   b should start work early and finish early.
   c should start work late and finish late.

Are you allergic to mornings?

Are you somebody who can't wake up in the morning? Do you need two cups of coffee before you can start a new day? Do you feel awful when you first wake up? Scientists say it's all because of our genes. How did they find this out? Researchers from the University of Surrey interviewed 500 people. They asked them questions about their lifestyle, for example what time of day they preferred to do exercise and how difficult they found it to wake up in the morning. Scientists then compared their answers to the people's DNA.

They discovered that we all have a 'clock' gene, also called a Period 3 gene. This gene can be long or short. People who have the long gene are usually people who are very good in the morning, but who get tired quite early at night. People who have the short gene are usually people who are more active at night but who have problems waking up early in the morning. How does it help us to know if we have the long or short gene? Scientists say that, if possible, we should try to change our working hours to fit our 'body clock'. If you are a 'morning person' then you could start work early and finish early. But if you are bad in the mornings, then it might be better to start work in the afternoon and work until late at night. So maybe, instead of nine to five it should be seven to three or twelve to eight.

Adapted from a British newspaper

4 LISTENING & SPEAKING

a **8.6** Listen to David being interviewed by a researcher. Is he a morning or evening person?

b Listen again and write down David's answers.

1 What do you do?
2 When do you work?
3 What time do you get up in the morning?
4 If you have an exam, do you study best in the morning, afternoon, or at night?
5 If you do exercise, when do you prefer to do it?
6 Do you like your working hours? (school/university timetable)?
7 Why (not)?
8 Would you like to change them (it)? How?

c Interview your partner using the questions in **b**. Is he / she a morning or evening person?

5 PRONUNCIATION   /g/ and /dʒ/

a How is the letter *g* pronounced in these words? Put five words in each column.

gene   get   go   change   energetic
gym   good   give   hungry   age

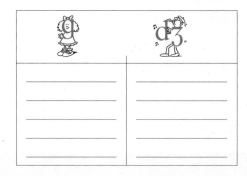

b **8.7** Listen and check. Practise saying the words.

c Now practise saying the sentences.
   1 She gets up early to go to the gym.
   2 George and Greta are good at German.
   3 I'm allergic to mornings. It's in my genes.
   4 I generally feel hungry and energetic.

6 **8.8** SONG ♫ *Say a little prayer*

8
D
G *so, neither* + auxiliaries
V similarities
P vowel and consonant sounds, sentence stress

I like dogs.
So do I.

'I'm Jim.' 'So am I.'

1 LISTENING

a Look at the photos and describe the two men.

b Read about the two men and answer the questions.

1 Who are Jim Springer and Jim Lewis?
2 Why didn't they know each other?
3 When did they meet?

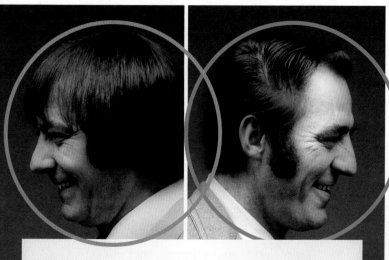

Some years ago, two identical twins were born in Minnesota USA. They were adopted by two different families. The two new families both called their babies Jim. **Jim** Springer never knew that **Jim** Lewis existed. But when they were 40 years old they met for the first time and they had a conversation something like this...

c **8.9** Cover the dialogue. Listen once. Try to remember **three** things they have in common.

d Uncover the dialogue. Listen again and fill the gaps.

A Hi! I'm Jim.

B So _____ I. Great to meet you. Are you married, Jim?

A Yes…well, I've been married twice.

B Yeah? So _____ I. Do you have any children?

A I have one son.

B So _____ I. What's his name?

A James.

B That's amazing! My son's name is James too.

A Did you go to university, Jim?

B No, I didn't.

A Neither _____ I. I was a terrible student.

B So _____ I. What do you like doing in your free time, Jim?

A I like making things, especially with wood.

B That's incredible! So _____ I.

A But I don't do any exercise at all. Look at me.

B Don't worry. Neither _____ I.

A Do you smoke?

B Yes. I smoke Salem cigarettes.

A So _____ I! What car do you have?

B A Chevrolet.

A Me too! Let's go and have a drink. What beer do you drink?

B Miller Lite.

A So _____ I!

2 GRAMMAR *so, neither* + auxiliaries

a Look at the dialogue again. Write one phrase that the twins use…

when they have something ⊞ in common. _____
when they have something ⊟ in common. _____

b ⟳ **p.140 Grammar Bank 8D.** Read the rules and do the exercises.

3 READING & VOCABULARY

a Read the text and answer the questions.

1 Who reunited the two Jims?
2 What did Dr Bouchard want to find out?
3 What was he very surprised by?
4 What are their sons and their dogs called?
5 What do they both do for their wives?
6 What does Dr Bouchard believe, as a result of the case of the two Jims?

b Complete the phrases with these words.

| as | both | like | neither | so | similar |

Similarities

1 Jim Springer looks exactly _____ Jim Lewis.
2 Jim Springer's son has the same name _____ Jim Lewis's son.
3 The two Jims _____ have dogs.
4 Jim Springer likes baseball and _____ does Jim Lewis.
5 Jim Lewis doesn't like basketball and _____ does Jim Springer.
6 Dr Bouchard didn't expect them to be so _____ to each other.

c Complete the sentences about you and your family. Tell your partner.

1 I have the same colour eyes as my _____.
2 I look like my _____.
3 My personality is quite similar to my _____'s.
4 My _____ and I both like _____.
5 I like _____ and so does my _____.
6 I don't like _____ and neither does my _____.

JIM SPRINGER AND JIM LEWIS were reunited after forty years by Dr Thomas Bouchard, Professor of psychology at the University of Minnesota. He was investigating how much of our personality depends on genes. Dr Bouchard was amazed by how many things the twins had in common. He had expected them to look identical and to have similar medical histories. But he and his team were very surprised to find the enormous similarities in the two Jims' personalities, their lifestyle, their hobbies, their religion, even their political beliefs.

Some of the similarities are incredible: Jim Springer's son is called James Allen, and Jim Lewis's is called James Alan. They both have dogs named Toy. They like and hate the same sports and they voted for the same President. And both Jims have the same romantic habit of leaving little love letters for their wives around the house.

Dr Bouchard is convinced that genes are probably much more important in determining our personality and preferences than people used to think.

4 PRONUNCIATION sounds, sentence stress

a The same or different? Circle the word with a different sound in each group.

1	so	no	do
2	they	neither	both
3	two	twice	twins
4	identical	incredible	immediately
5	food	good	wood
6	now	know	how
7	speak	great	each
8	beer	free	weekend

b **8.10** Listen and check. Practise saying the words.

c **8.11** Listen and repeat the dialogues. <u>Underline</u> the stressed words.

1 **A** I like tea.   **B** So do I.
2 **A** I'm tired.   **B** So am I.
3 **A** I don't smoke.   **B** Neither do I.
4 **A** I'm not hungry.   **B** Neither am I.

d **8.12** Listen and respond. Say you're the same. Use *So _____ I / Neither _____ I.*

5 SPEAKING

a Complete the sentences so they are true for you.

ME	WHO ELSE?
I love _____. (a kind of music)	_____
I don't like _____. (a TV programme)	_____
I'm _____. (star sign)	_____
I'm not very good at _____. (a subject)	_____
I'm going to _____ this weekend. (an activity)	_____
I have to _____ every day. (an obligation)	_____
I don't eat _____. (a kind of food)	_____
I'm not very _____. (adjective of personality)	_____

b Move around the class saying your sentences. For each sentence try to find someone like you, and write down their name. Respond to other people's sentences. Say *So do / am I* or *Neither do / am I* if you are like them.

I love classical music.
So do I.

CHECKING OUT

8.13 Listen to Allie talking to the receptionist. Answer the questions.

1 When is she leaving the hotel?
2 When does she want to pay?
3 What time is her flight?
4 What time does she have to be at the airport?
5 What is the message for her?

MAKING PHONE CALLS

a **8.14** Cover the dialogue and listen. Who does Allie want to speak to? What happens the first time she calls? Is the news good or bad? What is it?

YOU HEAR	YOU SAY
Hello.	Hello. Is that MTC?
Sorry, you've got the _____ number.	Oh sorry.
MTC New York. How can I help you?	Hello. Can I speak to Lisa Formosa, please?
Just a moment. I'll _____ you _____.	
Hello.	Hi, is that Lisa?
No, I'm sorry. She's not at her desk right now.	Can I leave a message, please?
Sure.	Tell her Allie Gray called. I'll call back in five minutes.
MTC New York. How can I help you?	Hello. Can I speak to Lisa Formosa, please?
Just a moment. I'm sorry, the line's _____. Do you want to _____?	OK, I'll hold.
Hello.	Hi Lisa. It's Allie Gray.
Allie, hi. How's California?	Great, great. Well? Is it good news or bad news?
It's good. You got the job in Paris!	Oh wonderful! That's fantastic!

b Listen again and complete the **YOU HEAR** phrases.

c **8.15** Listen and repeat the **YOU SAY** phrases. <u>C</u>opy the <u>rh</u>ythm.

d In pairs, roleplay the dialogue. **A** (book closed) you're Allie, **B** (book open) you're all the other people. Swap roles.

SOCIAL ENGLISH   saying goodbye?

a **8.16** Listen and mark the sentences T (true) or F (false).
1 Mark thinks that their relationship has a future.
2 She thinks it's a problem that Mark is very different from her.
3 Mark tells Allie he's going to move to another company.
4 Allie is very surprised.
5 Allie is going to be Mark's wife.

b Complete the **USEFUL PHRASES**. Listen again and check.

c **8.17** Listen and repeat the phrases. How do you say them in your language?

USEFUL PHRASES

A Thanks for e_____.
M C_____! To us.
A What do you m_____?
M I_____ that amazing?
M What's the m_____?
M I don't b_____ it.

a Read the article and complete it with these words.

| above all | although | another | ~~but~~ | general | however | secondly | which | who |

The weekend

The good side

For me the first good thing about the weekend is that I don't have to go to work. I like my job, ¹ _but_ I have to spend all day inside, in an office, and I'm a person ² _____ loves being outside. ³ _____ good thing is that I don't have to get up early. During the week I have to get up at half past six every day. It's not too bad in the summer but I hate it in the winter when it's dark in the morning. But ⁴ _____, I like the weekend because I have time to do all the things I really enjoy doing, like listening to music, reading, or going out with friends.

The bad side

⁵ _____, there are some things I don't like about the weekend. Firstly, I have to go shopping on Saturday morning, and the supermarket is always crowded. ⁶ _____, on Sundays we always have lunch with my husband's family. ⁷ _____ my mother-in-law is a good cook and her food is delicious, I don't usually have a good time. The family always argue and we end up watching TV, ⁸ _____ I think is boring.

But in ⁹ _____ I love the weekend – I often get a bit depressed on Sunday afternoon when I know that the weekend is nearly over.

b Read the article again. Now cover it and, from memory, mark the sentences T (true) or F (false).

1 She works outside.
2 She has to get up early during the week.
3 She enjoys shopping on Saturdays.
4 Her husband always makes lunch on Sundays.
5 She doesn't like watching TV.

What do you think of the weekend? **WRITE** two paragraphs.

Paragraph 1   **The good side**
For me the best thing about the weekend is…

Paragraph 2   **The bad side**
However, there are some things I don't like. For example,…

Final paragraph   Do you love it or hate it?
But in general,…

CHECK your article for mistakes (grammar , punctuation , and spelling).

8 What do you remember?

GRAMMAR

Circle the correct answer, a, b, or c.

What's _____ name?

a yours   (b) your   c you

1 **A** What did you do this weekend?
  B _____
  a Nothing.
  b Nobody.
  c Anything.

2 We didn't go _____ on Sunday.
  a somewhere
  b anywhere
  c nowhere

3 She spoke to _____ in the office.
  a anybody
  b somebody
  c nobody

4 He eats _____ crisps and chips.
  a too
  b too much
  c too many

5 I can't go. I'm _____ busy.
  a enough
  b too
  c too much

6 You don't drink _____.
  a water enough
  b enough water
  c a few water

7 Here are your shoes. Put _____.
  a on them
  b them on
  c it on

8 I can't find my keys. Can you help me _____?
  a look them for
  b look for them
  c for them look

9 **A** My father loves jazz.
  B _____
  a So I do.
  b So am I.
  c So do I.

10 **A** I didn't go to university.
   B _____
   a Neither do I.
   b Neither did I.
   c Neither I did.

10

VOCABULARY

a adjectives ending -ed and -ing

Complete the sentences with an adjective.

The film was very e*xciting* .

1 We had a very r_____ holiday – we just lay in the sun.
2 I only got three hours' sleep – I'm really t_____.
3 I saw a really i_____ TV programme last night.
4 She failed all her exams, so she feels a bit d_____.
5 My job's very b_____ – I have to do all the photocopying.

b health and lifestyle verbs

Complete the sentences with a verb.

She _drinks_ a lot of coffee.

1 I don't _____ enough exercise.
2 You should _____ sunscreen if you're going to the beach.
3 He _____ too many biscuits.
4 I _____ my friends every weekend.
5 You should _____ smoking, it's a terrible habit.

c phrasal verbs

Complete the sentences with a verb.

I _get_ up at 7.00.

| get look (x2) put turn wake |

1 Please _____ off the TV when you go to bed.
2 You should _____ up new words in a dictionary.
3 _____ up. It's 7.00.
4 _____ on a coat. It's cold.
5 I have to _____ after my little brother today.

15

PRONUNCIATION

a Underline the word with a different sound.

1	something	nobody	nothing	somebody
2	nobody	not	spoken	home
3	magazine	energetic	investigate	get up
4	neither	they	both	these
5	speak	great	each	meat

b Underline the stressed syllable.

infor<u>ma</u>tion

| somebody | relax | diet | enough | identical |

10

CAN YOU UNDERSTAND THIS TEXT?

Born to run

The Ethiopian runner, Haile Gebreselassie, the 'Emperor', is probably the greatest athlete of all time. He has won two Olympic titles, seven world titles and has broken numerous world records at 5,000 and 10,000 metres. A Sunday Times journalist went to interview him at his home in Addis Ababa.

Haile's routine has not changed since he became an athlete. Every morning he gets up at 5.45 and runs for two hours. He has a nap after lunch and then goes out running again.

Haile was brought up in a very poor family. Although today he is a multi-millionaire he has never been comfortable with being a rich man in such a poor country. 'The thing that really offends me,' he says, 'is that the most important value in the 21st century is how much money you have.'

In the future, when he retires from athletics, Haile may go into politics. 'I want to do something to help the people of Ethiopia. I have travelled to many countries. I have experience and I want to share that experience.' What Haile can't understand is why Europe is so rich and Ethiopia so poor. 'I was in Germany a week ago and it was freezing! Minus five. We have a much better climate. But we don't have enough water and so we don't have enough food and there are too many people.'

As we drive through the city in his ten-year-old Mercedes everybody recognizes him and shouts his name. A lorry carrying soldiers waits to let us pass. 'Even the army are your fans,' I say. 'No,' replies Haile. 'That was because there is a white man sitting in the front seat of the car with me.'

Adapted from a British newspaper

a Read the article and mark the sentences T (true), F (false), or DS (doesn't say).

1 Haile Gebreselassie is a long-distance runner.
2 He runs twice a day.
3 He enjoys being rich.
4 His family are also very rich.
5 He can't understand why Europe is richer than his country.
6 The soldiers stop because Haile is famous.

b Find a word or phrase in the article which means:

1 a short sleep (paragraph 1)
2 looked after when he was young (paragraph 2)
3 give something you have to other people too (paragraph 3)
4 very cold (paragraph 3)
5 calls in a loud voice (paragraph 4)

CAN YOU UNDERSTAND THESE PEOPLE?

a **8.18** Listen and circle the correct answer, a, b, or c.

1 Where did the woman go at the weekend?
   a to the cinema   b nowhere   c to the beach
2 The man doesn't eat enough _____.
   a fruit   b fish   c vegetables
3 How often does the woman go to the gym?
   a only on Friday   b twice a week   c every day
4 What time does the woman get up?
   a 7.00   b 7.15   c 7.30
5 What do the men have in common?
   a They drink coffee.   b They used to be married.
   c They're teachers.

b **8.19** Listen and write M (the man), W (the woman), or B (both).

Who…?

1 went to bed late   ___
2 is good in the mornings   ___
3 went to Liverpool University ___
4 studied Economics   ___
5 knows Fiona   ___

CAN YOU SAY THIS IN ENGLISH?

a Can you…? Yes (✓)

☐ talk about why you like / don't like the weekend
☐ talk about your lifestyle (food, exercise, etc.)
☐ talk about your typical morning

b Tell your partner about food you like / don't like. Find three things you have in common.

9 A

G past perfect
V adverbs: *suddenly*, *immediately*, etc.
P revision of vowel sounds, sentence stress

What a week!

> She had left the door open
> so the man went into her house.

Fact is always stranger than fiction.

Here is a selection of true stories from around the world last week.

Prize of the week.

1 James Bolton, who is unemployed, was very excited when he won first prize in a raffle last week. The prize was a weekend for two at a hotel in Bournemouth on the south coast of England. Unfortunately, he was less excited when he saw the name of the hotel. ☐

Mistake of the week

2 A 33-year-old Norwegian man came home one night from the pub and got into bed next to his wife. The woman immediately woke up, screamed, and jumped out of bed. 'Who are you?' asked the man. 'You aren't my wife.' ☐

Helpful advice of the week

3 An Italian was driving along the motorway when his cousin phoned him on his mobile. He told him to drive more slowly, because the police were waiting a few kilometres ahead to catch drivers who were going too fast. The driver slowed down, but two kilometres later the police stopped him and gave him a fine. ☐

Animal story of the week

4 Nurse Katie Parfitt from Manchester couldn't understand why her cat was behaving so strangely. The cat came home, attacked her bed, and then jumped on her plate while she was having her dinner. Then it fell asleep and began snoring. The next day when she spoke to her neighbour the mystery was solved. ☐

Honest citizen of the week

5 A man in Baltimore was arrested last week when he tried to become a policeman. When he filled in his application form for the job, he answered 'yes' to the question, 'Have you ever committed a crime?' ☐

Romantic hero of the week

6 The passengers on a German bus were amazed when their driver suddenly stopped the bus, got out, and began hitting a man who was making a phone call in a public phone box. First, the bus driver hit the man twice. Then the other man hit the bus driver very hard with the phone. The passengers were left sitting in the bus, and the bus driver was taken to hospital. ☐

Adapted from a British newspaper

1 SPEAKING & READING

a Look at the pictures 1–6 on p.100. In which picture can you see…?

somebody **screaming** ☐
someone getting a **fine** ☐
somebody winning a **raffle** ☐
something **snoring** ☐
somebody being **arrested** ☐
some passengers looking **amazed** ☐

b Read the stories and look at the pictures. Then in pairs, match them with their endings A–F.

> A They had seen him using his mobile phone while he was driving.

> B He had discovered the day before that his wife was having an affair with the man in the phone box.

> C When they questioned him, the man admitted he had stolen a car a few months before and had robbed five people in Texas.

> D The neighbour had seen it earlier that evening in the local pub. One of the customers had given it a drink of rum. Luckily, it has not become an alcoholic!

> E It was the hotel where he had worked as a porter the previous month. He had lost his job there.

> F The man had accidentally gone into his neighbour's house. The neighbour had left the back door open as she was waiting for her husband to come home.

c Read the stories again. Look at the pictures. Can you remember the stories?

2 GRAMMAR past perfect

a Look at these sentences from story 3. Answer the questions.
   a The police stopped the Italian driver.
   b They had seen him using his mobile phone.

   1 Which action happened first, **a** or **b**?
   2 What's the form of the verb in sentence **b**?

b Read the endings of the other five stories again and underline examples of *had* + past participle. Did these actions happen *before* or *after* the main part of the story?

c ⊙ **p.142 Grammar Bank 9A.** Read the rules and do the exercises.

3 PRONUNCIATION vowel sounds, sentence stress

a What sound do the pink letters make in each sentence? Match the sentences with the sound pictures.

A   B   C   D   E   F

   1 He suddenly understood why his brother hadn't come. ☐
   2 I didn't know Linda hadn't written since the spring. ☐
   3 The police had seen me in the street. ☐
   4 Paul thought the train had left at four forty. ☐
   5 We hadn't heard a word about the third murder. ☐
   6 We'd waited for ages to see the famous painting. ☐

b ⬤ **9.1** Now listen and repeat the sentences. Copy the rhythm, and practise making the sounds.

4 VOCABULARY adverbs

a Circle the adverbs in these five sentences from the stories in **1**. Underline the stressed syllable. Which two are opposites?

> The man had accidentally gone into his neighbour's house.

> Unfortunately, he was less excited when he saw the name of the hotel.

> The passengers were amazed when their driver suddenly stopped the bus.

> Luckily, it has not become an alcoholic!

> The woman immediately woke up, screamed, and jumped out of bed.

b Complete the sentences with one of the adverbs.

   1 I _____ took the office keys home with me.
   2 They were having a relaxed dinner when _____ the baby started to cry.
   3 The boss left, and _____ everyone started talking again.
   4 _____, the weather was terrible when we were on holiday.
   5 Last week I had a car crash. _____, nobody was hurt.

c In pairs, invent completions of these sentences.

   1 She got to work very late. Luckily…
   2 I was watching a good film on TV when suddenly…
   3 When we got out of the car it was raining. Unfortunately, we…
   4 I got home, had a shower, and immediately…
   5 I'm really sorry about the book you lent me. I accidentally…

5 SPEAKING

⊙ **Communication** *What had happened?* A p.111 B p.115. Try to say your partner's sentences.

9 B

G reported speech
V *say, tell,* or *ask*?
P rhyming verbs

> He said that he loved me.

Then he kissed me

1 SPEAKING & LISTENING

Then he kissed me

ask	dance	say	walk (x2)	want

1 Well, he ¹ _walked_ up to me and he ² _____ me if I ³ _____ to dance.
   He looked kind of nice and so I ⁴ _____ I might take a chance.
   When he ⁵ _____ he held me tight
   And when he ⁶ _____ me home that night
5 All the stars were shining bright
   And then he kissed me.

can't	don't know	is	say	see

Each time I ⁷ _____ him I ⁸ _____ wait to see him again.
I wanted to let him know that he ⁹ _____ more than a friend.
I ¹⁰ _____ just what to do
10 So I whispered 'I love you'
   And he ¹¹ _____ that he loved me too
   And then he kissed me.
   He kissed me in a way that I've never been kissed before,
   He kissed me in a way that I wanna be kissed forever more.

ask	feel	give	know	take

15 I ¹² _____ that he was mine so I ¹³ _____ him all the love that I had
   And one day he ¹⁴ _____ me home to meet his mum and his dad.
   Then he ¹⁵ _____ me to be his bride
   And always be right by his side
   I ¹⁶ _____ so happy I almost cried
20 And then he kissed me.

a Number the pictures A–H in a logical order.

b Complete the song with the verbs in the past simple. Use the glossary to help you.

c **9.2** Listen and check. Were your pictures in the right order?

Glossary

L.2 He looked kind of nice	He looked like a nice boy.
L.2 take a chance	try something to see if you are lucky
L.3 hold somebody tight	put your arms around somebody strongly
L.5 shining bright	with a very strong light
L.14 wanna	want to

2 GRAMMAR reported speech

A 'I love you too.'

B 'Do you want to dance?'

C He said he loved me too.

D He asked me if I wanted to dance.

a Look at the sentences. In pairs, answer the questions.

1 Which sentences are the speaker's exact words (direct speech)? ☐ ☐

2 Which sentences describe what the speaker said (reported speech)? ☐ ☐

3 What tense are the verbs in direct speech? p_____ simple

4 What tense are the verbs in reported speech? p_____ simple

b ⟳ **p.142 Grammar Bank 9B.** Read the rules and do the exercises.

c Change these sentences from direct speech to reported speech.

1 'My name's Dean.'   He said that *his name was Dean*.

2 'Do you want a drink?'   He asked her if _____.

3 'I'm not thirsty.'   She said _____.

4 'Will you go out with me?' He asked _____.

5 'Can I walk you home?'   He asked _____.

6 'Where do you live?'   He asked _____.

7 'I live quite near.'   She said _____.

8 'I fell in love at first sight.' He told Millie _____.

3 VOCABULARY *say, tell*, or *ask*?

Complete the sentences with *said*, *told*, or *asked*.

1 Jane _____ me if I could lend her some money.

2 I _____ him that I couldn't meet him tonight.

3 I _____ that I was too busy to go out.

4 We _____ the man if he could help us.

5 Annie _____: 'I have a problem.'

6 Annie _____ us that she had a problem.

7 She _____ her husband that she was leaving him.

8 He _____ the teacher that he had forgotten his homework.

4 PRONUNCIATION rhyming verbs

a Match a verb in the past tense from **A** with a rhyming one in **B**.

b ◯ **9.3** Listen and check.

A	B
said	crossed
paid	read
caught	wore
lost	stood
spent	meant
told	played
saw	sold
heard	bought
could	preferred

5 SPEAKING

a Choose and tick (✓) five questions below to ask your partner. Ask your questions and write down his / her answers.

Do you like flying?

What's your favourite colour? ☐

Can you play a musical instrument? ☐

Do you like flying? ☐

Where are your parents from? ☐

How long have you lived here? ☐

What languages do you speak? ☐

What kind of computer do you have? ☐

Do you have any phobias? ☐

Where do you buy your clothes? ☐

b Change partners. Tell partner 2 what you asked partner 1 and what his / her answers were.

I asked him what his favourite colour was and he told me that it was blue.

FILE 5 Grammar Bank p.134

In pairs or small groups, circle a, b, or c.

1 He went to the supermarket _____ some milk.
   a for to get   b for get   c to get
2 We're thinking of _____ a new office.
   a opening   b to open   c open
3

Tomorrow's a holiday. We _____ work.

   a don't must to   b mustn't   c don't have to
4 You _____ remember to bring your book tomorrow.
   a must to   b must   c have
5 He _____ the stairs and opened the door.
   a ran   b up   c ran up

FILE 6 Grammar Bank p.136

In pairs or small groups, circle a, b, or c.

1 What will you do if you _____ the exam?
   a won't pass   b don't pass   c will pass
2 If we had a garden, I _____ a dog.
   a would buy   b bought   c 'll buy
3 I wouldn't camp near a river if I _____ there were crocodiles there.
   a would thought   b thought   c think
4 A What are you going to do this weekend?
   B I don't know. I _____.
   a might to go away   b might go away
   c may to go away
5 You _____ coffee late at night.
   a shouldn't to drink   b don't should drink
   c shouldn't drink

FILE 7 Grammar Bank p.138

In pairs or small groups, circle a, b, or c.

1 I've known my best friend _____.
   a since ten years   b for ten years   c for 1995
2 How long _____ your car?
   a do you have   b have you   c have you had
3 He's divorced now, but he _____ for 20 years.
   a has been married   b was married
   c is married
4 He _____ have a lot of friends at school. He wasn't very popular.
   a didn't used to   b didn't use to
   c doesn't use to
5 The radio _____ by Marconi.
   a invented   b is invented   c was invented

FILE 8 Grammar Bank p.140

In pairs or small groups, circle a, b, or c.

1 When I'm tired I don't want to see _____.
   a anybody   b nobody   c somebody
2 I can't come tonight. I've got _____ work.
   a too many   b too much   c too
3 I don't eat _____. I should eat more.
   a fruit enough   b some fruit   c enough fruit
4 There's a towel on the floor. Please _____.
   a pick up   b pick it up   c pick up it
5 A I hate football.
   B _____
   a So am I.   b So do I.   c Neither do I.

FILE 9 Grammar Bank p.142

In pairs or small groups, circle a, b, or c.

1 We were too late. When we arrived the match _____.
   a had finished   b has finished   c finished
2 They couldn't open the door because they _____ the key.
   a didn't brought   b hadn't brought   c haven't brought
3 'I love you.' She said she _____ me.
   a love   b loved   c is loving
4 I asked her if _____ to dance.
   a he wanted   b she wants   c she wanted
5 She asked the boy what _____.
   a was his name   b is his name   c his name was

Vocabulary

Do the exercises in pairs or small groups.

a Circle the word that is different.

	car	train	(station)	bus
1	funny	friendly	lazy	generous
2	eye	mouth	nose	toe
3	feet	legs	knees	fingers
4	see	hear	ear	smell
5	foggy	windy	sunny	cloudy
6	dress	cap	skirt	blouse
7	socks	trainers	pyjamas	boots
8	get an e-mail	get a message	get home	get a present
9	duck	chicken	butterfly	swan
10	dolphin	whale	eagle	shark

b Complete the phrases.

> carry   do   get   go   know   make
> meet   spend   sunbathe   wear

1 _____ on the beach
2 _____ a coat
3 _____ a bag
4 _____ a noise
5 _____ yoga
6 _____ somebody for a long time
7 _____ somebody for the first time
8 _____ swimming
9 _____ angry
10 _____ time (with your friends)

c Complete with *on, up,* etc.

1 I was born _____ 2nd April.
2 What are you doing _____ the weekend?
3 We always go on holiday _____ July.
4 I don't agree _____ you.
5 Wait _____ me. I'm nearly ready.
6 Don't throw _____ those papers.
7 I always try _____ clothes before I buy them.
8 Hurry _____. We're late.
9 I have to look _____ my little sister today.
10 I'll pay you _____ the money tomorrow.

d Write the opposite verb or adjective.

1 friendly _____
2 talkative _____
3 crowded _____
4 rude _____
5 patient _____
6 lend money _____
7 pass an exam _____
8 push the door _____
9 find your keys _____
10 buy clothes _____

e Label the pictures.

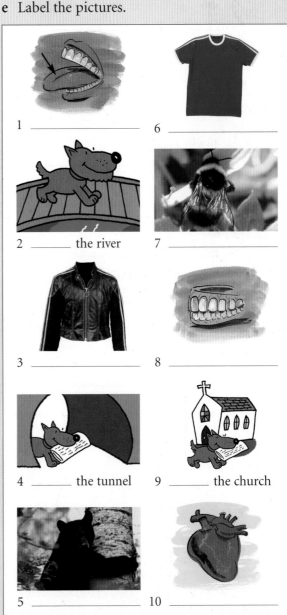

1 _____   6 _____
2 _____ the river   7 _____
3 _____   8 _____
4 _____ the tunnel   9 _____ the church
5 _____   10 _____

Pronunciation

Do the exercises in pairs or small groups.

a Underline the word with a different sound.

1	↑	nothing	enough	mouse	mustn't
2		shoes	trousers	through	few
3		since	tidy	might	neither
4		many	already	friends	secret
5		although	clothes	come	most
6		won't	want	borrow	body
7		worn	shirt	dirty	worst
8		mouth	how	slowly	round
9		awful	ball	story	work
10		fast	pass	ask	walk
11		who	hour	holiday	hate
12		age	just	enjoy	glasses
13		gym	argue	forget	goal
14		used	yet	years	eyes
15		which	where	twin	two

b Underline the stressed syllable.

information

1 biography
2 exercise
3 university
4 divorced
5 borrow
6 decision
7 always
8 promise
9 dangerous
10 polite
11 towards
12 afraid
13 education
14 interesting
15 along
16 important
17 anything
18 depressing
19 language
20 unfortunately

c Write the words.

1 /ʃʊd/ _____
2 /kwaɪt/ _____
3 /luːz/ _____
4 /ɔːlˈðəʊ/ _____
5 /ˈtiːtʃə/ _____
6 /ˈnʌθɪŋ/ _____
7 /ˈrɪəli/ _____
8 /ˈhaʊswɜːk/ _____
9 /ɪnˈdʒɔɪ/ _____
10 /lɑːf/ _____

107

Communication

5A Guess the infinitive **Student A**

a Look at sentences 1–6. What do you think the missing infinitives are?
Don't write anything yet!

$+$ = positive infinitive $-$ = negative infinitive

1 I don't like my job. I've decided _____ another one. $+$
2 Oh dear! I forgot _____ the lights. $+$
3 I promise _____ anybody your secret. $-$
4 Your sister's really friendly. It was very nice _____ her. $+$
5 I was sorry _____ you when you were here last week. $-$
6 You don't need _____ an umbrella. It's not going to rain. $+$

b Read your sentence 1 to **B**. If it's not right, guess another verb until **B** says 'That's right'. Then write in the infinitive. Continue with 2–6.

c Listen to **B**'s sentence 7. If it's the same as 7 below, say 'That's right'. If not, say 'Try again' until **B** gets it right. Continue with 8–12.

7 Remember **to phone** your father on his birthday.
8 It's often difficult **to understand** films in English.
9 It's a very formal dinner, so it's important **not to be** late.
10 I'm going to Australia **to visit** some friends.
11 The jacket was really expensive so I decided **not to buy** it.
12 My mobile number is very easy **to remember**.

6C Decisions, decisions **Student A**

a Imagine that you are a very indecisive person. **B** is going to ask you some questions. Answer **B**'s questions. Give two possibilities each time using *I may* or *I might*. Then **B** will help you to make a decision.

> I don't know. / I'm not sure. I might… or I may…

b Swap roles. Now **B** is indecisive. Ask **B** question 1 below. Help **B** to make a decision using *If I were you, I'd …* Say why. Continue with the other questions.

1 Where are you going to go on holiday next summer?
2 What are you going to do after class?
3 What are you going to wear tomorrow?
4 What are you going to buy when you next go shopping?
5 Where are you going to have lunch on Sunday?

Communication

7D Passives quiz Student A

a Complete your sentences with the verb in the passive and the right answer.

1 **Until 1800 New York** _____ (call) _____.
   a New Amsterdam   **b** New Hampshire   **c** New Liberty

2 **Chess** _____ (invent) by _____.
   a the Egyptians   **b** the Indians   **c** the Chinese

3 **The Italian flag** _____ (design) by _____.
   a Garibaldi   **b** Mussolini   **c** Napoleon

4 **The first Levi jeans** _____ (wear) by _____.
   a miners   **b** farmers   **c** cowboys

5 **The first credit card** _____ (use) in _____.
   a 1960   **b** 1970   **c** 1980

6 **The Indiana Jones films** _____ (direct) by _____.
   a Steven Spielberg   **b** George Lucas   **c** Stanley Kubrick

7 **Penguins** _____ (find) _____.
   a at the South Pole   **b** at the North Pole   **c** in Alaska

8 **In the world 15,000 babies** _____ (be born) _____.
   a every second   **b** every hour   **c** every day

b Read your sentences to **B**. **B** will tell you if you are right.

c Now listen to B's sentences. Tell him / her if he / she is right.

B's answers
1 The CD player was invented by Philips.
2 The *Star Wars* films were directed by George Lucas.
3 The politician Winston Churchill was born in a toilet.
4 The book which is stolen most often from libraries is *The Guinness Book of Records*.
5 The electric chair was invented by a dentist.
6 Football was first played by the British.
7 In 1962 the original London Bridge was bought by a rich American.
8 The noun which is used most frequently in conversation is *time*.

9A What had happened? Student A

a Look at sentences 1–6 and think of the missing verb (+ = positive verb, − = negative verb). **Don't write anything yet!**

1 Diana was very angry because her husband _____ the dinner. −

2 He couldn't catch his plane because he _____ his passport at home. +

3 We went back to the hotel where we _____ on our honeymoon. +

4 The telephone wasn't working because they _____ the bill. −

5 Miriam was surprised to hear that she _____ the exam. +

6 The shop assistant agreed to change the sweater, because I _____ it. −

b Read your sentence 1 to **B**. If it's not right, try again until **B** tells you 'That's right'. Then write in the verb. Continue with 2–6.

c Listen to B say sentence 7. If it's the same as 7 below, say 'That's right'. If not say 'Try again' until **B** gets it right. Continue with 8–12.

7 We went back to see the house where we **had lived** when we were children.

8 The flat was very dirty because nobody **had cleaned** it for a long time.

9 The crocodile was hungry because it **hadn't eaten** anything for a long time.

10 I ran to the station, but the last train **had gone**.

11 I didn't want to lend him the book because I **hadn't read** it.

12 They got to the cinema late and the film **had started**.

8B Body age Students A+B

a Start with your calendar age. Add + or subtract − years according to your answers.

1	**a** −2	**b** −1	c 0	**d** +1
2	**a** −2	**b** −1	c −1	**d** +2
3	**a** +2	**b** +1	c 0	**d** −1
4	**a** +1	**b** −1	c −2	
5	**a** −2	**b** −1	c +1	
6	**a** +1	**b** +1	c +2	**d** 0
7	**a** −3	**b** +1	c +5	
8	**a** −3	**b** +1	c +2	
9	**a** + 3	**b** 0	c −2	
10	**a** −2	**b** 0	c −1	
11	**a** −2	**b** −1	c 0	**d** +2
12	**a** +2	**b** +1	c −1	

5A Guess the infinitive   **Student B**

a   Listen to **A** say sentence 1. If it's the same as 1 below, say 'That's right'. If not, say 'Try again' until **A** gets it right. Continue with 2–6.

   1   I don't like my job. I've decided **to look for** another one.
   2   Oh dear! I forgot **to turn off** the lights.
   3   I promise **not to tell** anybody your secret.
   4   Your sister's really friendly. It was very nice **to meet** her.
   5   I was sorry **not to see** you when you were here last week.
   6   You don't need **to take** an umbrella. It's not going to rain.

b   Look at sentences 7–12. What do you think the missing infinitives are? **Don't write anything yet!**

   + = positive infinitive   − = negative infinitive

   7   Remember _____ your father on his birthday. +
   8   It's often difficult _____ films in English. +
   9   It's a very formal dinner, so it's important
        _____ late. −
  10   I'm going to Australia _____ some friends. +
  11   The jacket was really expensive, so I decided
       _____ it. −
  12   My mobile number is very easy _____ . +

c   Read your sentence 7 to **A**. If it's not right, guess another verb until **A** says 'That's right'. Then write in the infinitive. Continue with 8–12.

Communication

6C Decisions, decisions **Student B**

a **A** is a very indecisive person. You are going to help him / her make some decisions. Ask **A** question 1 below. Help **A** to make a decision using *If I were you, I'd …* Say why. Continue with the other questions.

1 What's the next film you're going to see?
2 What are you going to cook for dinner tonight?
3 What are you going to do on Saturday night?
4 What car are you going to buy next?
5 How are you going to celebrate your next birthday?

b Swap roles. Now imagine that <u>you</u> are a very indecisive person. Answer **A**'s questions. Give two possibilities each time using *I may* or *I might* … **A** will help you to make decisions.

> I don't know. / I'm not sure. I might… or I may…

7D Passives quiz **Student B**

a Complete your sentences with the verb in the passive and the right answer.

1 **The CD player _____ (invent) by _____ .**
   a Sanyo   **b** Sony   **c** Philips

2 **The *Star Wars* films _____ (direct) by _____ .**
   a George Lucas   **b** Steven Spielberg   **c** Stanley Kubrick

3 **The politician Winston Churchill _____ (be born) _____ .**
   a on a train   **b** in a toilet   **c** under a bridge

4 **The book which _____ (steal) most often from libraries is _____ .**
   a The Bible   **b** *The Guinness Book of Records*   **c** *The Lord of the Rings*

5 **The electric chair _____ (invent) by _____ .**
   a a teacher   **b** a dentist   **c** a politician

6 **Football _____ first _____ (play) by _____ .**
   a the British   **b** the Romans   **c** the Greeks

7 **In 1962 the original London Bridge _____ (buy) by _____ .**
   a a rich American   **b** a museum   **c** the Royal family

8 **The noun which _____ (use) most frequently in conversation is _____ .**
   a *money*   **b** *time*   **c** *work*

b Now listen to **A**'s sentences. Tell him / her if they are right.

A's answers
1 Until 1800 New York was called New Amsterdam.
2 Chess was invented by the Chinese.
3 The Italian flag was designed by Napoleon.
4 The first Levi jeans were worn by miners.
5 The first credit card was used in 1970.
6 The Indiana Jones films were directed by Steven Spielberg.
7 Penguins are found at the South Pole.
8 In the world 15,000 babies are born every hour.

c Read your sentences to **A**. **A** will tell you if you are right.

9A What had happened? **Student B**

a Listen to **A** say sentence 1. If it's the same as 1 below, say 'That's right.' If not say, 'Try again' until **B** gets it right. Continue with 2–6.

1 Diana was very angry because her husband **hadn't cooked** the dinner.
2 He couldn't catch his plane because he **had left** his passport at home.
3 We went back to the hotel where we **had stayed** on our honeymoon.
4 The telephone wasn't working because they **hadn't paid** the bill.
5 Miriam was surprised to hear that she **had failed** the exam.
6 The shop assistant agreed to change the sweater because I **hadn't worn** it.

b Look at sentences 7–12 and think of the missing verb (⊞ = positive verb, ⊟ = negative verb). **Don't write anything yet!**

7 We went back to see the house where we _____ when we were children. ⊞
8 The flat was very dirty because nobody _____ it for a long time. ⊞
9 The crocodile was hungry because it _____ anything for a long time. ⊟
10 I ran to the station, but the last train _____ . ⊞
11 I didn't want to lend him the book because I _____ it. ⊟
12 They got to the cinema late and the film _____ . ⊞

c Read your sentence 7 to **A**. If it's not right, try again until **A** tells you 'That's right'. Then write in the verb. Continue with 8–12.

5D Cross country **Students A+B**

a You are the organizer of a cross-country race. You have to plan the race for the runners. Draw a route on the map marked **MY RACE**, beginning at **START** and finishing at the **FINISH** line. Your route <u>must</u> include all the things in the picture but you can choose the order.

b Take turns. A describe your route to your partner.
B must draw it on your map marked **MY PARTNER'S RACE**.

> You have to go down the hill, round the lake...

c Swap roles.

d Compare the two routes. Which is the most difficult?

Listening

5.1

1

Harry Hello, you're one of Peter's friends aren't you?

Adrian That's right. I'm Adrian.

Harry Hi, I'm Harry. Are you enjoying the party?

Adrian Yes.

Harry So, what do you do for a living, Adrian?

Adrian I'm a doctor.

Harry A doctor? Oh that's good. Listen, I have a problem with my back. Could you have a look at it? I've got a pain just here…

Adrian Sorry, can you excuse me? I've just seen Peter over there and I want to wish him a Happy Birthday.

2

Man James, this is Sandra.

James Hi.

Sandra Nice to meet you.

Man Sandra's a teacher in secondary school.

James A teacher? Really? What a wonderful job! You're so lucky!

Sandra Why lucky?

James Well, you have really long summer holidays!

Sandra Yes, that's what people always say. Perhaps you would like to teach my class one day. When you teach teenagers all year you *need* a long summer holiday.

3

Catherine Hello. We haven't met before, have we?

Luke No, I don't think so.

Catherine I'm Catherine, I'm Peter's sister.

Luke Oh, hi, I'm Luke. I went to school with Peter.

Catherine Ah, Luke! You're the travel agent, aren't you?

Luke Yes, I am.

Catherine Peter's told me all about you. Listen, can you recommend a cheap holiday? I'd like to go somewhere hot. And I want to go in August. But when I say cheap, I mean cheap. Oh and I can't fly…because I'm terrified of flying…

4

Woman Deborah, can I introduce you to an old friend of mine, Lucy?

Deborah Hi Lucy.

Lucy Nice to meet you.

Woman Lucy's my hairdresser.

Deborah Ah. You're just the person I want to talk to, Lucy. What do you think of my colour?

Lucy Well…

Deborah No, come on, tell me the truth. Is it too blonde?

Lucy Er… no. I think it's fine.

Deborah Are you sure?

Woman Lucy, what would you like to drink?

Lucy Oh, a Diet Coke please.

Deborah Do you think my hair would look better shorter?

Woman Deborah, Lucy's not at work now.

Deborah Oh sorry.

5

Andrea Hi. I'm Andrea. Nice to meet you.

Simon Hello. My name's Simon.

Andrea What do you do Simon? No, don't tell me! Let me guess your job! Let me see. You look like a … professional footballer.

Simon No… I'm a psychiatrist.

Andrea A psychiatrist! Ooh how fascinating! Simon…? Are you analysing me?

Simon Er, no, I'm not. Excuse me, er, Andrea. I need to go to the bathroom.

5.5

Interviewer Good evening and welcome. In today's programme we're going to talk about singing. In the studio we have Martin, the director of a singing school in London and Gemma a student at Martin's school. Good morning to both of you.

Martin & Gemma Good morning.

Interviewer First Martin, can you tell us, why is it a good idea for people to learn to sing?

Martin First, because singing makes you feel good. And secondly because singing is very good for your health.

Interviewer Really? In what way?

Martin Well, when you learn to sing you need to learn to breathe correctly. That's very important. And you also learn to stand and sit correctly. As a result, people who sing are often fitter and healthier than people who don't.

Interviewer Are your courses only for professional singers?

Martin No, not at all. They're for everybody. You don't need to have any experience of singing. And you don't need to be able to read music.

Interviewer So how do your students learn to sing?

Martin They learn by listening and repeating. Singing well is really 95% listening.

Interviewer OK, Gemma. Tell us about the course. How long did it last?

Gemma Only one day. From ten in the morning to six in the evening.

Interviewer Could you already sing well before you started?

Gemma No, not well. But I have always liked singing. But I can't read music and I never thought I sang very well.

Interviewer So what happened on the course?

Gemma Well, first we did a lot of listening and breathing exercises and we learnt some other interesting techniques.

Interviewer What sort of things?

Gemma Well, for example we learnt that it is easier to sing high notes if you sing with a surprised look on your face!

Interviewer Oh really? Could you show us?

Gemma Well, I'll try.

Interviewer For those of you at home, I can promise you that Gemma looked *very* surprised. Were you happy with your progress?

Gemma Absolutely. At the end of the day we were singing in almost perfect harmony. It was amazing. In just one day we really were much better.

Interviewer Could you two give us a little demonstration?

Martin & Gemma Oh, OK.

5.7

I arrived at Kraków airport with Kasia, my guide. Test number one. I had to get a taxi to the hotel. I said to the taxi driver, in Polish, 'To the Holiday Inn hotel, please,' – *Prosze do hotelu Holiday Inn*. No problem. The driver understood me. But then he started talking to me in perfect English. I felt a bit stupid.

We got to the hotel, checked in, and then we went to the hotel bar for test number two.

A waitress came up to us and I said '*Prosze piwo*', that is, a beer please. Then the waitress said something in Polish and I understood her! She said 'a big or small beer?' 'Big,' I said. I was so happy that I could understand her. I really enjoyed that beer.

Next we went out into the street for test three: asking for directions. I decided to ask for directions to a chemist, because I knew the word for chemist, *apteka*. I stopped a woman who looked friendly and I said, in Polish, 'Excuse me please, is there a chemist's near here? No problem. But then she started talking really fast and pointing. I tried to listen for left or right or anything I could understand but no, I couldn't understand anything. I was sure that Kasia was going to give me zero for this test!

I was feeling less confident now. We went back to the hotel for test four: making a phone call. Kasia gave me a phone number and told me to ask to speak to her friend. His name was Adam. I dialled the number. A woman answered the phone. 'Is Adam there?', I said hopefully. '*Adama nie ma*,' she said. I understood that! Adam's not in. I wanted to say 'When will he be back?' but I could only say 'When home? '*Kiedy domu*?' And I didn't understand her answer. So I said thank you and goodbye very politely. Kasia smiled, so I thought, well, not bad.

Finally, test five: asking the time. I *knew* this test was going to be very hard. Numbers in Polish are incredibly difficult and I've always found telling the time is impossible. But I had a brilliant idea. I stopped a man in the street and said, 'Excuse me, what's the time?' I couldn't understand the answer but I just said, 'Sorry, can I see your watch please?' He showed it to me. Twenty past seven. Perfect!

How well did I do in the tests? Well, Kasia gave me five out of ten for language and eight for imagination. So can you learn a language in a month? Not Polish, definitely!

SA Can I help you?

Allie Yes, I really like this sweater. Do you have it in a medium?

SA Let's see… we have it in red in a medium.

Allie No, I want it in black.

SA Just a minute, I'll go and check. Here you are. A black medium. Do you want to try it on?

Allie No, thanks. I'm sure it'll be fine. How much is it?

SA 43.38.

Allie It says 39.99.

SA Yes, but that doesn't include sales tax – that's 8.5% extra.

Allie Oh, OK. Do you take MasterCard?

SA Yes, of course.

Mark Allie! You look great, as usual. How was your morning?

Allie Really good. First I went shopping, and then I went to the Museum of Modern Art.

Mark What did you think of it?

Allie It was wonderful. But I didn't have enough time to see it all. Never mind.

Mark Maybe next time.

Allie What a lovely evening!

Brad Hi, Allie. How was the shopping?

Allie Great, thanks.

Brad Hi Mark. And did you like the museum? I hope you didn't get lost again!

Mark Hey, I didn't know you two were friends already.

Allie We met this morning. I got lost. I was trying to find Union Square – and suddenly Brad appeared.

Brad So I took her to my favourite coffee shop.

Mark Allie, what would you like to drink?

Allie I'd like a cocktail please. A margarita.

Brad What a good idea. I'll have one too. Mark, could you get us a couple of margaritas?

Mark Oh, so now I'm the waiter, am I?

Brad So tell me about the museum, Allie. What was your favourite painting?

Interviewer OK, Michael, can you tell us what to do in these three situations? First what about the crocodile attack?

Michael Well, once a crocodile has seen you it will attack you, so doing nothing is not really an option. And a crocodile attacks so quickly that people never have time to swim to safety. The crocodile will try to get you in its mouth and take you under the water. Your only hope is to try to hit it in the eye or on the nose. If you did this and you were very lucky the crocodile would open its mouth and give you time to escape. But I have to say that it's very difficult, although not impossible, to survive a crocodile attack.

Interviewer What about the bear attack?

Michael When a bear attacks someone, their natural reaction is always to try to run away or to climb up a tree. But these are both bad ideas. Bears can run much faster than we can and they're also much better and faster at climbing trees.

The best thing to do in this situation would be to pretend to be dead. A bear usually stops attacking when it thinks that its enemy is dead and so, if you were lucky it would lose interest in you and go away.

Interviewer And finally, the bull attack?

Michael Well, if you were in the middle of a field, forget about running. Bulls can run incredibly fast. And don't shout or wave your arms because bulls react to movement and this will just make the bull come in your direction. The best thing to do is to try not to move, and just stay where you are, and then at the last moment to throw something, a hat or your shirt, away from you. If you were lucky, the bull would change direction to follow the hat or shirt and you'd be able to escape. By the way, it doesn't matter what colour the shirt is. It isn't true that bulls like red. They don't see colour, they only see movement.

Presenter Welcome to this morning's edition of *What's the problem?*. Today we're talking about friends, so if you have a problem with one of your friends, call us now. And if you're listening to the programme and you think you can help with any of the problems then just send an e-mail to our website. Our e-mail address is what.problem@radiotalk.com. Our first caller today is Barbara. Hello Barbara.

Barbara Hello.

Presenter What's the problem?

Barbara Well, I have a problem with a friend called Jonathan (that's not his real name). Well, Jonathan often goes out with me and my friends. The problem is that he's really mean.

Presenter Mean?

Barbara Yes, he never pays for anything. When we have a drink he always says he doesn't have any money or that he's forgotten his money. So in the end one of us always pays for him. At first we thought, 'Poor Jonathan, he doesn't have much money'. But it's not true. His parents work, and he works on Saturdays in a shop – so he must have some money. Do you think we should say something to him?

Presenter Thanks Barbara. I'm sure you'll soon get some e-mails with good advice. OK, our next caller is Kevin from Birmingham. Hello Kevin.

Kevin Hi.

Presenter What's the problem?

Kevin Yes. My problem is with my best friend. Well, the thing is, he's always flirting with my girlfriend.

Presenter Your best friend flirts with your girlfriend?

Kevin Yes, when the three of us are together he always says things to my girlfriend like, 'Wow! You look fantastic today,' or 'I love your dress, Suzanna,' things like that. And when we're at parties he often asks her to dance.

Presenter Do you think he's in love with your girlfriend?

Kevin I don't know, but I'm really angry about it. What can I do?

Presenter Well, let's see if one of our listeners can help, Kevin. And our last caller is Catherine. OK Catherine, over to you. What's the problem?

Catherine Hello. I'm at university and I live on the university campus. I live in a flat and I share a room with this girl. She's really nice. I get on very well with her, but there's one big problem.

Presenter What's that?

Catherine She always borrows things from me without telling me.

Presenter What does she borrow?

Catherine Well, first it was CDs and books, but now she's started taking my clothes as well, sweaters, jackets, and things. Yesterday she took a white sweater of mine and she didn't tell me. So when I wanted to wear it this afternoon it was dirty. I don't want to lose her as a friend but what should I do?

Presenter Thank you Catherine. So… if you can help Barbara, Kevin, or Catherine, e-mail us at…

Receptionist Hi. How can I help you?

Allie Do you have any painkillers? I have a headache.

Receptionist I'm sorry. We can't give our guests medicine. But we can call a doctor for you if you like.

Allie No, it's OK. I don't need a doctor. It's just a cold. But is there a chemist's near the hotel?

Receptionist Do you mean a pharmacy?

Allie Sorry, that's right, a pharmacy.

Receptionist Sure. There's one right across the street.

Allie Thank you.

Receptionist You're welcome.

Mark Bless you! Are you OK?

Allie It's just a cold. I had a bad headache this morning, but I feel better now.

Mark Listen. I'm really sorry about last night.

Allie What do you mean?

Mark At the party. I got kind of angry at Brad. He was really annoying me.

Allie Oh, I think he's very nice.

Mark Yeah, women always think so.

Allie Don't worry, Mark. Brad's not my type.

Mark So what is your type, Allie?

Allie You know what my type is. Dark hair, 34 years old, lives in San Francisco…

Mark Listen, tomorrow's your last day. I want to do something special. What would you like to do?

Allie I don't mind. You choose.

Mark How about a boat trip around the bay? We could do that in the morning, and then have a nice dinner in the evening.

Allie That sounds fantastic.

Mark It's too bad you can't stay longer.

Allie Yes, it's a pity – this week has gone so quickly. I feel I've just arrived and now I'm going home.

Mark Well, I'm going to make sure tomorrow is a really special day.

7.1

Interviewer What exactly is your phobia, Scott?

Scott Well, the medical name is Felinophobia or Gatophobia.

Interviewer And what does that mean exactly?

Scott It means I'm afraid of cats.

Interviewer Cats?

Scott Yes.

Interviewer How long have you had this phobia?

Scott Since I was a child.

Interviewer And how did it start?

Scott When I was five or six years old, I remember going to a friend's house and I saw a cat on the stairs. And the cat was looking at me, well staring at me. I went to touch it, and it bit me. And since then I've always been afraid of cats.

Interviewer What happens if you see a cat?

Scott Well, I start to feel very nervous, my hearts beats quickly. And I have to go away very quickly from where the cat is. For example, if I see a cat in the street, I always cross to the other side.

Interviewer What do you do?

Scott I'm a doctor.

Interviewer Is your phobia a problem for you in your work?

Scott Yes, sometimes. For example, if I go to a house and there is a cat I have to ask the people to put the cat in another room. I can't be in the same room as a cat.

Interviewer Have you ever had any treatment for your phobia?

Scott Yes, I've just started going to a therapist. I've had three sessions.

Interviewer How's it going?

Scott Well, now I can look at a photo of a cat without feeling nervous or afraid. And I can touch a toy cat. The next step will be to be in a room with a real cat.

Interviewer Do you think you will ever lose your phobia of cats?

Scott I hope so. I'm optimistic. Who knows, maybe one day I'll have a cat as a pet.

7.5

Presenter Good evening and welcome to *Film of the week*. Tonight we are going to see Sofia Coppola's film *Lost in Translation*. This film came out in 2003, and it gave the young film director her

first Oscar nomination. Before it starts, Anthony, can you tell us a bit about her?

Anthony Well, of course as you know, Sofia Coppola is the daughter of Francis Ford Coppola, so you could say that she was born with a camera in her hand. She was born in New York in 1971 while her father was making the film *The Godfather*, and in fact she actually appeared in the film – she was the little baby in the baptism scene.

After she left school she decided to become an actress, but her career as an actress didn't last long. When her father made *The Godfather part III*, he gave his daughter a part in the film. She played Mary Corleone, the Godfather's daughter. But it was a disaster and the film critics wrote terrible things about her. So she stopped being an actress and she went to the California Institute of Art where she studied fine arts and photography. Then she decided to become a film director.

1999 was a really big year for her. She directed her first film, *The Virgin Suicides*, and this time the critics thought she was great. She also got married, to the film director Spike Jonze – but they separated after a few years.

And then in 2003 she made her next film, which is the one we're going to see now called *Lost in Translation*. *Lost in Translation* was the film which made Sofia Coppola famous. For this film she became the first American woman to be nominated for an Oscar for best director, although she didn't win it.

Presenter Thank you very much Anthony. And now, let's watch *Lost in Translation*.

7.6

Interviewer How old are you in the photograph, Melissa?

Melissa Twelve or thirteen, I think.

Interviewer Did you like school?

Melissa Not really.

Interviewer Why not?

Melissa Because I didn't like any of the subjects. Well, that's not quite true, I liked English, but that was the only lesson I used to look forward to. I didn't like maths, didn't like science at all, and I *hated* PE. I used to argue with the PE teacher all the time. She used to make us do impossible things, things we couldn't do, like climbing ropes and jumping over the horse. I think she just wanted to humiliate us.

Interviewer Were you a 'good girl' at school?

Melissa It depends what you mean by 'good'. I didn't smoke, I didn't use to write graffiti on the walls or anything like that. But I was a bit of a rebel. I used to break rules all the time, and of course the teachers didn't like that.

Interviewer What sort of rules did you break?

Melissa Well, the school was very strict about the school uniform – we had to

wear a blue skirt, and the skirt had to cover our knees. I used to make the skirt shorter. And then I sometimes used to wear blue socks and a black sweater, like in the photograph instead of a grey sweater, and grey socks. The teachers used to get really angry; I just thought it was silly.

Interviewer What did you want to be when you were at school?

Melissa I wanted to be a lawyer.

Interviewer Why?

Melissa Well, there were a lot of American TV programmes and films about lawyers at the time, and I used to think it would be fun to argue with people all day.

Interviewer So why did you become a primary school teacher?

Melissa Lots of reasons. But I think the main reason is that both my parents were teachers and they both used to tell me, when you grow up and get a job *don't* be a teacher. So as I was a rebel, I did exactly the opposite.

7.11

Presenter Good afternoon, and welcome to another edition of *Science Today*. In today's programme we are going to hear about women inventors. When we think of famous inventors we usually think of men, people like Alexander Graham Bell, Guglielmo Marconi, Thomas Edison. But as Sally will tell us, many of the things which make our lives easier today were invented by women.

Sally That's absolutely right. Let's take the dishwasher for example. This was invented by a woman called Josephine Cochrane in 1886. She was a rich American who gave a lot of dinner parties. But she was annoyed that her servants used to break plates and glasses when they were washing them after the party. So, Josephine decided to try and invent a machine which could wash a lot of plates and glasses safely. Today the dishwasher is used by millions of people all over the world.

The car was invented by a man, but it was a woman, Mary Anderson, who in 1903 solved one of the biggest problems of driving. Until her invention, it was impossible for drivers to see where they were going when it was raining or snowing. The name of her invention? Windscreen wipers.

A fantastic invention that definitely improved the lives of millions of people was disposable nappies. They were invented by a woman called Marion Donovan in 1950. Anybody who has a small baby will know what a big difference disposable nappies make to our lives. Today more than 55 million nappies are used every day in the world.

A few years later in 1956, Bette Nesmith Graham was working as a secretary. She used to get very frustrated and angry when she made typing mistakes. In those days if you made a mistake you had to get a new sheet of paper and start again from the beginning. She had a brilliant idea, which was to use a white liquid to paint over mistakes. Her invention is called Tipp-Ex today. Mrs Graham was a divorced mother and her invention made her a very rich woman.

And finally… policemen, soldiers, and politicians all over the world are protected by something which was invented by a woman. In 1966 Stephanie Kwolek invented kevlar, a special material which was very light but incredibly strong, much stronger than metal. This material is used to make the bullet-proof vest. Her invention has probably saved thousands of lives.

Presenter Thanks very much Sally. So… if you thought that everything was invented by men, think again.

7.14

Mark Hi, Allie. How are you feeling today?
Allie Much better.
Mark Good. Are you going to be warm enough with just that sweater? It might be a little cold on the boat.
Allie I'll be fine. Are we going to walk to the bay?
Mark No, it's too far. It's better if we get a cab.
Allie How long does it take by cab?
Mark About ten minutes.
Allie And how long's the boat trip?
Mark I'm not sure. I think it's an hour. Why?
Allie Well, I have to be back here by 1.00 – I'm expecting an important phone call.
Mark Not from Brad, I hope?
Allie Well, actually… No, of course not! From the New York office.
Mark OK. Let's go.

7.17

Mark So, what do you think of San Francisco?
Allie It's beautiful, Mark. I love it.
Mark Better than London?
Allie Not better. Different.
Mark Do you think you could live here?
Allie No, I don't think so.
Mark Oh. Why?
Allie Well, it's a long way from London. I think I'd miss all my family and friends.
Mark Could you live somewhere else – but in *Europe*?
Allie Maybe. Why do you ask?
Mark Oh, no reason. I just wondered.
Tannoy *On your left you can see the island of Alcatraz.*
Mark Look, can you see that building? That used to be the prison, but it was closed in 1963. It's a museum now.
Allie Where are we going for dinner tonight?
Mark It's a surprise.
Allie I'm really looking forward to it.
Mark Me too.
Allie Brr. I'm cold.
Mark Do you want to borrow my coat?

Allie No. It's OK. I'm going to miss you, Mark.
Mark Hey, excuse me! Could you take a photo of us, please?
Man Sure. Are you ready?
Allie Ready.
Man Say cheese!

8.3

Newsreader Last Friday Sven, a company lawyer from Stockholm was looking forward to a relaxing two days in the mountains. He and his wife had booked a skiing weekend in a luxury hotel. But the weekend didn't work out exactly as they had planned. Sven worked until late on Friday evening. His office was on the 12th floor. When he finished, at 8 o'clock, he locked his office and got into the lift…and he didn't get out again until Monday morning!
Sven I pressed the button for the ground floor and the lift started going down but then stopped. I pressed the button again but nothing happened. I pressed the alarm and shouted but nobody heard me. Most people had already gone home. I tried to phone my wife but my mobile didn't work in the lift… I couldn't do anything. I just sat on the floor and hoped maybe somebody would realize what had happened. But on Saturday and Sunday I knew nobody would be there. I slept most of the time to forget how hungry I was.
Newsreader Meanwhile Sven's wife, Silvia was waiting for her husband to come home.
Silvia I was very worried when he didn't come home on Friday evening and I couldn't understand why his mobile wasn't going. I phoned the police and they looked for him but they couldn't find him anywhere. I thought maybe he was with another woman.
Newsreader So Sven was in the lift the whole weekend from Friday evening until Monday morning. At eight o'clock, when the office workers arrived, they phoned the emergency number and somebody came and repaired the lift.
Sven I was very happy to get out. I hadn't eaten since Friday afternoon and I was very hungry. It's lucky that I am not claustrophobic because the lift was very small. The first thing I did was to phone my wife to say that I was OK.
Newsreader Sven will soon be the fittest man in his office – from now on he's going to take the stairs every day – even though it's 12 floors.

8.6

Interviewer Hello. Could I ask you a few questions? We're doing some research.
David Sure. What's it about?
Interviewer Well, we want to find out if you are a morning or an evening person.
David OK, fine.
Interviewer OK and what's your name?

David David Cope.
Interviewer And, what do you do, David?
David I'm a magazine editor.
Interviewer OK, and when do you work?
David Monday to Friday, eight till four.
Interviewer What time do you get up in the morning?
David 5.45. I have to get up early because I start work at 8 and it takes me an hour to get to work.
Interviewer What time do you go to bed?
David Probably around 10.00.
Interviewer If you have an exam, do you study best in the morning, afternoon, or at night?
David Let me think, I haven't done an exam for a long time but when I was a student I used to study better in the morning.
Interviewer And…if you do exercise when do you prefer to do it?
David In the morning, definitely. I love going for a long walk or cycling. It's great early in the morning because you feel that you're the only person in the world who's awake at that time.
Interviewer Do you like your working hours?
David I don't mind them. Finishing work early means I can pick up my daughter from school, and look after her in the afternoons. It's true that I can't really have a social life during the week, because I go to bed at ten, but that's OK.
Interviewer Right, and the last question. Would you like to change your working hours?
David Yes, I would. I'd like to work four days a week, maybe working more hours in the day and have a three-day weekend. Then I could spend three full days a week with my family.
Interviewer That's great. Thank you very much for your time.

8.13

Receptionist Good afternoon. How can I help you?
Allie Hi. I'm leaving tomorrow morning very early. Could you prepare my bill so I can pay this evening?
Receptionist Of course.
Allie And could you order me a cab?
Receptionist For what time?
Allie My flight's at 9.15, so I have to be at the airport at 7.15.
Receptionist Then you'll need a cab at six o'clock. I'll order one for you.
Allie Thanks. Oh, and has there been a phone call for me?
Receptionist Oh yes. There's a message for you. Can you call this number in New York?
Allie Right. Thanks.
Receptionist You're welcome.

5

5A uses of the infinitive (with *to*)

infinitive + *to*

> I want **to go** to the party.
> I need **to buy** some new clothes.
> It'll be nice **to meet** some new people.
> It's important **not to be** late.

- Use *to* + the infinitive after:
  – some verbs (*want, need, would like*, etc.) See **Verb Forms** p. 154.
  – adjectives
  It isn't easy to find a job. Nice to meet you.
- The negative infinitive is *not to* + verb.
  Try not to be late tomorrow.

infinitive of purpose

> **A** Why did you go to the party?   **B To meet** new people.
> I went to the party **to meet** new people.

- Use *to* + the infinitive to say why you do something.
  I came to this school to learn English. NOT ~~for learn English~~.

5B verb + *-ing*

> **Eating** outside in the summer makes me feel good.
> I love **reading** in bed.
> I'm thinking of **buying** a new car.

- Use verb + *ing*:
  – as the subject of a sentence
  Smoking is bad for you.
  – after some verbs, (*like, love, hate, enjoy*, etc.) See **Verb Forms** p. 154.
  I hate getting up early.
  – after prepositions
  He left without saying goodbye.
- Remember the spelling rules for the *-ing* form (See p. 126 1C)

5C *have to, don't have to, must, mustn't*

have to, don't have to

+	She **has to** get up at 7.00 every day. You **have to** drive on the left in the UK.
−	We **don't have to** wear a uniform at this school. He **doesn't have to** work on Saturdays.
?	**Do** I **have to** buy a grammar book? **Does** she **have to** study tonight?

Don't contract *have* or *has*.
I have to go. NOT ~~I've to go.~~

- Use *have to* + infinitive to talk about rules and obligations, or to say something is necessary.
- Use *don't have to* + infinitive to say there is no obligation, or something is not necessary.
- Use *do / does* to make questions and negatives.
  Do I have to go? NOT ~~Have I to go?~~

must / mustn't

+	You **must** do your homework tonight. She **must** tidy her room before she goes out.
−	You **mustn't** smoke in class. They **mustn't** leave their bags here.

Contraction: *mustn't* = must not

- Use *must* + infinitive to talk about rules and obligations.
  You must turn off your mobile phones before coming into class.
- *must / mustn't* are the same for all persons. It is not often used in questions (*have to* is more common).
- Use *mustn't* + infinitive to say something is prohibited.
  You mustn't smoke here.
- You can use *mustn't* or *can't* to talk about rules.
  You mustn't park here. You can't park here.

> ⚠ *Must* and *have to* are very similar, but there is a small difference. We normally use *have to* for a general obligation (a rule at work or a law). We normally use *must* when the speaker imposes the obligation (for example, a teacher to students or a parent to children). But often you can use either.
>
> *Mustn't* and *don't have to* have completely different meanings. Compare:
> *You mustn't go* = You can't go. It's prohibited.
> *You don't have to go* = You can go if you want, but it's not obligatory/necessary.

5D expressing movement: *go*, etc. + preposition

> The man **went up** the steps and **into** the church.
> I **ran over** the bridge and **across** the park.
> He **drove out of** the garage and **along** the street.

- To express movement use a verb of movement, for example, *go, come, run, walk*, etc. and a preposition of movement (*up, down*, etc.)

- Be careful with *in / into* and *out / out of*. Use *into / out of* + noun, but if there isn't a noun just use *in* or *out*.
  *Come **into** the living room. Come **in**.*
  *He went **out of** the house. He **went out**.*

5A

a Complete with *to* + a verb.

I'm planning *to have* a holiday next month.

do not drive go learn leave not make meet

1 **A** Hi, I'm Dagmara.
  B I'm Renata. Nice _____ you.
2 What do you want _____ this evening?
3 I need _____ to the bank. I don't have any money.
4 Try _____ a noise. Your father's asleep.
5 I'd really like _____ a new language.
6 Be careful _____ too fast on the way home.
7 She's decided _____ her husband.

b Match the sentence halves.

They want to go to Australia	D	A	to celebrate getting the job.
1 He's going to have a party		B	to get some petrol.
2 You'll need a visa		C	to book our tickets.
3 Don't forget to phone the restaurant			
4 I stopped at the garage		D	~~to visit their family there.~~
5 She's gone to the supermarket		E	to tell them where we are.
6 I went to the travel agent's		F	to go to China.
7 I'll send them a text message		G	to book a table.
		H	to get some food for tonight.

5B

a Complete the sentences with a verb in the *-ing* form.

be ~~do~~ go learn remember study talk teach

I don't really enjoy *doing* exercise.
1 My mother's very bad at _____ names.
2 _____ teenagers is very hard work.
3 You can't sing well without _____ to breathe properly.
4 My sister spends hours on the phone _____ to her boyfriend.
5 I hate _____ the first to arrive at parties.
6 _____ by train is cheaper than by plane.
7 I'll go on _____ until dinner time.

b Put the verbs in the *-ing* form or infinitive.

I like *listening* to music. (listen)
1 _____ yoga is good for your health. (do)
2 We've decided _____ to the party. (not go)
3 We won't take the car. It's impossible _____. (park)
4 I'm not very good at _____ maps. (read)
5 You can borrow the car if you promise _____ slowly. (drive)
6 Have you finished _____ your homework? (do)
7 I don't mind _____ but I hate _____. (cook, wash up)

5C

a Write sentences with the right form of *have to*.

I / work on Saturday ⊟ *I don't have to work on Saturday.*

1 Jane / work very hard ⊞
2 you / wear a uniform ?
3 my sister / go to school ⊟
4 I / finish this now ?
5 we / get up early tomorrow ⊟
6 Harry / work tomorrow ?
7 we / hurry or we'll be late ⊞

b Complete the sentences with *have to*, *don't have to*, or *mustn't*.

We *don't have to* work tomorrow. It's a holiday.

1 You _____ touch those animals. They're dangerous.
2 We _____ take the bus to school. It's too far to walk.
3 The concert is free. You _____ pay.
4 It's late. I _____ go now.
5 You _____ leave the door open – the cats will come in.
6 You _____ come if you don't want to. I can go on my own.
7 In Britain you _____ drive on the left.
8 You _____ be very tall to play football.

5D

a Cross out the wrong preposition.

My mobile stopped working when we went **across** / **through** a tunnel.

1 She ran **to** / **down** the lake, and jumped **into** / **out of** the water.
2 If you go **over** / **past** the church, you'll see my house on the left.
3 He walked **along** / **across** the street until he got to the chemist's.
4 The plane flew **on** / **over** the town and then landed.
5 The policeman walked **towards** / **to** me, but then he stopped.
6 We drove **over** / **out of** the bridge and **in** / **into** the city centre.
7 The cyclists went **round** / **under** the track three times.

b Complete the sentences with *in*, *into*, *out*, or *out of*.

He jumped *into* his car and drove away.

1 I like to go _____ on a Friday night.
2 Come _____. The door's open.
3 He took his passport _____ his jacket.
4 He walked _____ the café and ordered a coffee.

6A   *if* + present, *will* + infinitive (first conditional)

> **If** I **miss** the bus, **I'll get** a taxi.
> She **won't be** angry **if** you **tell** her the truth.
> What **will** you **do if** it **rains**?

> ⚠ You can also use the imperative or *can*.
> *If you miss the bus, get a taxi.*
> *If you miss the bus, you can get a taxi.*

- Use *if* + present, *will* + infinitive to talk about a possible future situation and its consequence.
- The *if* clause can come first or second.
  I'll come if you like. OR *If you like, I'll come.*

6B   *if* + past, *would* + infinitive (second conditional)

> **If** a bear **attacked** me, **I'd run** away.
> **If** I **didn't have** children, I **wouldn't live** in the country.
> **Would** you **take** the manager's job **if** they **offered** it to you?

- Use *if* + past, *would* + infinitive to talk about an improbable / impossible or hypothetical future situation and its consequence.
  If a bear attacked me, I'd run away. = I'm imagining this situation. It's very improbable.
- *would* / *wouldn't* is the same for all persons.
- The contraction of *would* is *'d* (*I'd*, *you'd*, *he'd*, etc.) and of *would not* is *wouldn't*.

- The *if* phrase can come first or second.
  If I saw a bear, I'd run. OR *I'd run if I saw a bear.*
- Remember with *can*, use *could* + infinitive, not ~~would can~~.
  If I had a car, we could drive there.

> ⚠ With the verb *be* you can use *were* (instead of *was*) after *I* and *he* / *she* / *it*.
> *If he was / were here, he'd help you.*
> Use *were* (not *was*) in the expression *If I were you...*
> We often use this expression for advice.

First and second conditionals

Compare the first and second conditionals:
Use the **first conditional** for **possible** future situations.
If I have time tomorrow, I'll help you. (= maybe I will have time)
Use the **second conditional** for **improbable / impossible** or **hypothetical** situations.
If I had time tomorrow, I'd help you. (= I won't have time.)

6C   *may* / *might* + infinitive (possibility)

> We **might** have a picnic tomorrow, but it depends on the weather.
> I **might not** go to the party. I haven't decided yet.
> I **may** go to the party, but I'm not sure.
> I **may not** have time to do everything today.
>
> ***Might not*** and ***may not*** aren't usually contracted.

> ⚠ You can also use *May I... / May we...* to ask for permission.
> *May I use your phone?* (= can I use your phone).

- Use *might* / *may* and *might not* / *may not* +infinitive to talk about a future possibility.
  It might / may rain. = It's possible that it will rain.
- *Might / May* (*not*) is the same for all persons, *I might / may, he might / may, we might / may*, etc.

6D   *should* / *shouldn't* (advice)

> I think you **should** change your job.
> The government **should** do more for old people.

- Use *should* / *shouldn't* + infinitive to give somebody advice or say what you think is the right thing to do.
  You should cut your hair. = I think it would be a good idea.
- *should* / *shouldn't* + infinitive is the same for all persons.
- You can also use *ought to* / *ought not to* instead of *should* / *shouldn't*.
  You ought to change your job.

6A

a Match the sentence halves.

If you leave now	*C*	A if you don't start now.
1 It will be cheaper		B will you give it back to me?
2 If I don't see you later,		C ~~you'll catch the 8.00 train.~~
3 You'll learn more		D if you go by bus.
4 If you get the job,		E I'll see you on Friday.
5 You won't have time		F if you come to every class.
6 If I lend you this book,		G will you earn more money?

b Complete with the correct form of the verbs.

If you __tell__ me your secret, I _won't tell_ anybody. (tell, not tell)
1 If we _____ walking, the bus _____. (start, come)
2 He _____ angry if you _____ him. (be, not tell)
3 If I _____ it down, I _____ it. (not write, not remember)
4 _____ you _____ me if you _____ any news? (call, get)
5 If you _____ her nicely, she _____ you. (ask, help)
6 You _____ if you _____. (not pass, not study)

6B

a Match the sentence halves.

You'd feel much better	*C*	A we could go shopping.
1 I'd enjoy the weekend more		B I'd get a new job.
2 If you stayed for another day,		C ~~if you stopped smoking.~~
3 Would you wear it		D if I went to live in China?
4 If I were you,		E if I bought it for you?
5 I wouldn't work		F if I didn't need the money.
6 Would you come with me		G if I didn't have to work on Saturday.

b Complete with the correct form of the verbs.

If I _found_ a good job, I _would move_ to the USA. (find, move)
1 We _____ the house if it _____ a garden. (buy, have)
2 If I _____ his number, I _____ him. (know, phone)
3 You _____ more if you _____ harder. (learn, work)
4 If you _____ for a week, you _____ see everything. (stay, can)
5 We _____ our son more often if he _____ nearer. (see, live)
6 I _____ to the doctor's if I _____ you. (go, be)

6C

a Match the sentence halves.

Take your umbrella.	*D*	A You might fall.
1 Let's buy a lottery ticket.		B It might not be your size.
2 Phone the restaurant.		C We might get lost.
3 Don't stand on the wall.		D ~~It might rain.~~
4 Let's take a map.		E I might be late.
5 Try the shirt on.		F You might cut yourself.
6 Don't wait for me.		G It might be closed on Sundays.
7 Be careful with that knife.		H We might win.

b Complete the sentences with *may / might* + a verb.

be cold	be ill	be in a meeting	~~go to the cinema~~
not have time		not like it	win

I'm not sure what to do tonight. I _might go to the cinema._
1 Kate wasn't in class today. She _____
2 He isn't answering his phone. He _____
3 It's an unusual film. You _____
4 I don't know if I'll finish it. I _____
5 It's a difficult match but we _____
6 Take your coat. It _____

6D

a Complete with *should* or *shouldn't*.

You _should_ stop smoking.
1 You _____ eat red meat.
2 You _____ work 12 hours a day.
3 You _____ lose a bit of weight.
4 You _____ eat more fruit.
5 You _____ drink a lot of coffee.
6 You _____ put salt on your food.
7 You _____ start doing some exercise.

b Complete the sentences with *should* or *shouldn't* + a verb.

drive	go	~~leave~~	relax	study	walk	wear

We _should leave_ early. There might be a lot of traffic later.
1 You _____ a jacket. It's quite cold today.
2 I _____ tonight. I have an exam tomorrow.
3 You _____ alone in that part of the city. Get a taxi.
4 She _____ more. She's very stressed.
5 People _____ so fast when it's raining.
6 You _____ to bed early tonight. You look really tired.

7

7A present perfect + *for* and *since*

A Where do you live now?	**B** In Manchester.
A **How long have you lived** there?	**B** **I've lived** there **since** 1990.
A Where do you work?	**B** In a primary school.
A **How long have you worked** there?	**B** **I've worked** there **for** five years.

⚠ You can't use the present simple here.
NOT ~~How long do you live here?~~
~~I live in Manchester since 1980.~~

- Use the present perfect + *for* or *since* to talk about actions and states which started in the past and are still true now.
  I've lived in Manchester since 1990. = I came to live in Manchester in 1990 and I live in Manchester now.
- Use *How long?* to ask questions about the duration of an action or a state.

- Use *since* with the beginning of a period of time, for example, *since 1980, since last June,* etc.
  I've been afraid of water since I was a child.
- Use *for* + a period of time, for example, *for two weeks, for ten years,* etc.
  I've had this car for three months.

7B present perfect or past simple (2) ?

How long **has** Tarantino **been** a director?	He**'s been** a director since the 1980s.
How many films **has** he **made**?	He**'s made** six films.
How long **was** Hitchcock a director?	He **was** a director for 50 years.
How many films **did** he **make**?	He **made** 52 films.

⚠ Don't use *since* with the past simple.
NOT ~~He was Prime Minister since 1999.~~
You have to use *from…to*.
He was Prime Minister from 1999 to 2003.

- Use the present perfect + *how long?, for,* and *since* to talk about a period of time from the past until now.
  How long have you been married? I've been married for 10 years. (= I'm married now.)
- Use the past simple + *how long?* and *for* to talk about a finished period of time in the past.
  How long was he married? He was married for two years. (= He's not married now.)

7C *used to / didn't use to*

+	**−**
I You He She It We They **used to** wear glasses.	I You He She It We They **didn't use to** wear glasses.

?	**✔**	**✘**
Did I you he she we they **use to** wear glasses?	**Yes,** I you he she we they **did.**	**No,** I you he she we they **didn't.**

- Use *used to / didn't use to* + infinitive for things that happened repeatedly or over a long period of time in the past, but are usually <u>not</u> true now, for example for things which happened when you were a child.
  I used to have long hair. I used to play in the street. I didn't use to have a TV.
- You can also use the past simple here. *I had long hair when I was a child.*

⚠ *used to* only exists in the past.
Don't use *use to* for present habits.
Use the present simple + *usually*.
I usually cook in the evenings.
NOT ~~I use to cook in the evenings.~~

7D passive: *be* + past participle

Present

+	**−**	**?**
Risotto **is made** with rice.	It **isn't made** with pasta.	**Is** it **made** with meat?
These offices **are cleaned** every morning.	They **aren't cleaned** on Saturdays.	**Are** they **cleaned** on Sundays?

Past

+	**−**	**?**
Guernica **was painted** by Picasso.	It **wasn't painted** by Dali.	When **was** it **painted**?
The pyramids **were built** by the Egyptians.	They **weren't built** by the Greeks.	Why **were** they **built**?

- You can often say things in two ways, in the active or in the passive.
  Picasso painted Guernica. (**active**)   *Guernica was painted by Picasso.* (**passive**)
- In the active sentence, the focus is more on the person (e.g. Picasso).
- In the passive sentence the focus is more on the painting (e.g *Guernica*).
- You can also use the passive when it's not known or not important who does or did the action.
  My car was stolen last week. (I don't know who stole it.)

- Make the present passive with *am / is / are* + the past participle.
- Make the past passive with *was / were* + the past participle.
- Use *by* to say who did the action.
  The Lord of the Rings was written by Tolkien.

7A

a Write questions with *How long* and the present perfect.

you / be married   *How long have you been married?*

1 he / have his car _____ ?
2 your parents / lived in this house _____ ?
3 you / be a teacher _____ ?
4 she / know her boyfriend _____ ?
5 Poland / be in the EU _____ ?
6 you / have your dog _____ ?
7 Tim / be frightened of water _____ ?

b Answer the questions in a. Use the present perfect + *for* or *since*.

I've been married since 1986.

1 He _____ three years.
2 They _____ a long time.
3 I _____ 1990.
4 She _____ May.
5 It _____ 2004.
6 We _____ about two years.
7 He _____ he was a child.

7B

a Right (✔) or wrong (✗)? Correct the wrong sentences.

She is married since 1990. ✗ *She's been married since 1990.*

1 He has left school last year.
2 I lived in Brighton for two years, but then I moved to London.
3 She lives in Hollywood since 2004.
4 My sister has had her baby yesterday!
5 I work in a bank. I work there for twenty years.
6 The city has changed a lot since I was a child.
7 They're divorced now. They have been married for a year.

b Complete with the present perfect or past simple.

1 **A** Where does Joanna live now?
  B In Washington.
  A How long _____ there? (she / live)
  B For six months. She _____ there in February. (move)
2 **A** When _____? (Picasso / die)
  B In 1977, in Paris I think.
  A How long _____ in France? (he / live).
  B For a long time. He _____ Spain when he was 25. (leave)
3 **A** My sister and her husband get on very well.
  B How long _____ married? (they / be)

7C

a Look at how James has changed. Write five sentences about how he was **THEN**.

THEN

He didn't use to be slim.

1 _____ short hair.
2 _____ quite fat.
3 _____ glasses.
4 _____ a uniform.
5 _____ wine.

NOW

b Make sentences with *used to*, *didn't use to*, or *did … use to*.

you / have long hair ?
Did you use to have long hair?

1 where / you / go to school ?
2 I / like vegetables when I was a child −
3 my sister / hate maths at school +
4 what / you / do in the summer ?
5 they / live near here −
6 this building / be a cinema +
7 your brother / study here ?

7D

a Complete with present or past passive.

The Eiffel Tower *was built* in 1889. (build)

1 All the singer's clothes _____ specially for her. (make)
2 The grass _____ every month. (cut)
3 Australia _____ by Captain Cook in 1770. (discover)
4 This morning I _____ up by the neighbour's dog. (wake)
5 Cricket _____ in the summer in the UK. (play)
6 These songs _____ last year. (record)
7 Most children _____ in state schools. (educate)

b Rewrite the sentences in the passive.

Shakespeare wrote Hamlet in 1603.
Hamlet *was written by Shakespeare in 1603.*

1 Last night the police stopped us.
  Last night we _____.
2 American teenagers eat a lot of fast food.
  A lot of fast food _____.
3 Toulouse-Lautrec painted *At the Moulin Rouge.*
  At the Moulin Rouge _____.
4 The marketing manager organizes weekly meetings.
  Weekly meetings _____.
5 The Italians make Fiat cars.
  Fiat cars _____.

8

8A something, anything, nothing, etc.

	+	**?** and **−** verb	**✗** Short **−** answer
people	somebody someone	anybody anyone	nobody no one
things	something	anything	nothing
places	somewhere	anywhere	nowhere

Somebody's in the bathroom.   Is **anybody** in the bathroom?   There isn't **anybody** in the bathroom.

- Use *somebody, something, someone,* etc. when you don't say exactly who, what, or where.
  Somebody broke the window.
  I went somewhere nice at the weekend.
- Use *anything, anybody, anywhere* in questions or with a − verb.
  I didn't do anything last night. NOT *I didn't do nothing.*

- Use *nobody, nothing, nowhere* in short
  − answers or in a sentence (with a + verb).
  Who's in the bathroom?
  Nobody. Nobody's in the bathroom.
  NOT *Anybody is in the bathroom.*
- *Somebody, Nobody,* etc. are the same as *Someone, No one,* etc.

8B quantifiers

too, too much, too many

> I'm stressed. I have **too much** work.
> My diet is unhealthy. I eat **too many** cakes and sweets.
> I don't want to go out. I'm **too** tired.

- Use *too, too much, too many* to say 'more than is good'.
- Use *too* + an adjective NOT *I'm too much tired.*
- Use *too much* + uncountable nouns (e.g. coffee, time).
- Use *too many* + countable nouns (e.g. cakes, people).

enough

> Do you eat **enough** vegetables?
> I don't drink **enough** water.
> This dress isn't big **enough**.

- Use *enough* <u>before</u> a noun to mean 'all that is necessary'.
- Use *enough* <u>after</u> an adjective.

a little, a few

> **A** Do you take sugar?   **B** Yes. Just **a little**.
> **A** Do want some chips?   **B** Yes, but **just a few**.
> I eat **a little** meat.   Can you buy **a few** bananas?
> I drink **very little** coffee.   He has **very few** friends.

- Use *a little / very little* and *a few / very few* to talk about small quantities.
- Use *a little / very little* with uncountable nouns and *a few / very few* with countable nouns.

8C word order of phrasal verbs

> Every morning I **get up** at 8.00.
> Then I **turn on** the radio.
> I always have to **look for** my glasses.

- A phrasal verb = verb + particle (preposition or adverb) *get up, turn on, look for.*
  1 Some phrasal verbs don't have an object.
    Come in and *sit down.*
    What time do you get up?
  2 Some phrasal verbs have an object and are separable.
    Put on your coat.
    Turn off the TV.

- With these verbs you can put the particle (*on, off,* etc.) <u>before</u> or <u>after</u> the object.
  Put on your coat OR *Put your coat on.*
  Turn off the TV OR *Turn the TV off.*
- When the object is a pronoun (*me, it, him,* etc.) it <u>always</u> goes between the verb and particle.
  Here's your coat. Put it on. NOT *Put on it.*
  I don't want to watch TV. Turn it off. NOT *Turn off it.*
  3 Some phrasal verbs have an object and are inseparable.
    I'm looking for my keys.
    I'm looking for them.
  With these phrasal verbs, the verb (*look*) and the particle (*for*) are never separated.
  I looked after my little sister. NOT *I looked my little sister after.*
  I looked after her. NOT *I looked her after.*

8D so, neither + auxiliaries

> **A** I love football.
> **B** So do I.
> **A** I went to university.
> **B** So did I.
> **A** I'm not married.
> **B** Neither am I.
> **A** I don't smoke.
> **B** Neither do I.

- Use *So do I / Neither do I,* etc. to say that you have something in common with somebody.
- Use *So* + auxiliary + *I* with positive sentences.
  A *I'm happy.* **B** *So am I.* NOT *So I am.*
- Use *Neither* + auxiliary + *I* with negative sentences.
  A *I'm not hungry.* **B** *Neither am I.*
  NOT *Neither I am.*

- The auxiliary you use depends on the tense.
  I love football.   *So do I.*
  I didn't like the film.   *Neither did I.*
  I can swim.   *So can I.*
  I wasn't very tired.   *Neither was I.*
  I've been to Spain.   *So have I.*
  I wouldn't like to go there.   *Neither would I.*

8A

a Complete with *something, anything, nothing,* etc.

Did you meet ___anybody___ last night?

1 Are you doing _____ tonight?
2 _____ phoned when you were out. He said he'd call back later.
3 I've seen your car keys _____ but I can't remember where.
4 Did _____ come while I was out?
5 Did you go _____ exciting last night?
6 I've bought you _____ for your birthday.
7 I knocked at the door but _____ answered.
8 We went shopping but we didn't buy _____.

b Answer with *Nobody, Nowhere,* or *Nothing.*

1 What did you do last night? _____
2 Where did you go yesterday? _____
3 Who did you see? _____

c Answer the questions in **b** with a full sentence.

1 I didn't do _____
2 _____
3 _____

8B

a Cross out the wrong form.

How **much** / ~~many~~ meat do you eat?

1 I drink **too** / **too much** coffee.
2 I eat **too much** / **too many** biscuits.
3 I don't drink **enough water** / **water enough**.
4 I can't go. I am **too** / **too much** busy.
5 You work **too much** / **too many**.
6 I only drink **a few** / **a little** coffee.
7 I don't have **enough time** / **time enough**.
8 He has **a few** / **a little** good friends.

b Complete the sentences with *too, too much, too many,* or *enough.*

You eat _too much_ red meat. It isn't good for you.

1 My father's not very fit. He doesn't do _____ exercise.
2 I can't walk to work. It's _____ far.
3 There are _____ cars on the roads today.
4 I don't sleep _____ – only five or six hours, but I really need eight.
5 I was _____ tired to go out last night.
6 There were _____ people at the party, so it was impossible to dance.

8C

a Complete the sentences with a particle from the box.

after	away	back	down (x2)	for	~~off~~	on	up

Turn _off_ your mobile before you come into class. ✔

1 Turn _____ the radio. It's too loud.
2 What time do you usually get _____ in the morning?
3 John phoned when you were out. He'll call _____ later.
4 My brother is looking _____ a new job.
5 I think you should throw _____ those old jeans.
6 I always try _____ new clothes before I buy them.
7 I have to look _____ my little sister tonight.
8 You should write _____ new words in your book.

b Tick the sentences in **a** where the particle (*on, off,* etc.) could also go after the object.

c Complete the sentences with *it* or *them* and a particle.

away	off (x2)	on	up (x3)

1 I can't hear the radio. Turn _____ _____.
2 Your clothes are all over the floor. Pick _____ _____.
3 Here's your coat. Put _____ _____.
4 What does this word mean? Look _____ _____.
5 Your shoes are wet. Take _____ _____.
6 I don't need those papers. Throw _____ _____.
7 Don't watch the TV now. Turn _____ _____.

8D

a Complete **B**'s answers with an auxiliary verb.

A I like coffee.   **B** So _do_ I.

1 **A** I'm really hungry.   **B** So _____ I.
2 **A** I didn't go out last night.   **B** Neither _____ I.
3 **A** I was born in Liverpool.   **B** So _____ I.
4 **A** I don't smoke.   **B** Neither _____ I.
5 **A** I've been to Bangkok.   **B** So _____ I.
6 **A** I can't swim.   **B** Neither _____ I.
7 **A** I'd like to go to India.   **B** So _____ I.
8 **A** I saw a film last night.   **B** So _____ I.

b Respond to **A**. Say you are the same.
Use *So...I* or *Neither...I*

A I don't like whisky.   _Neither do I._

1 **A** I live near the school.   _____
2 **A** I'm not afraid of snakes.   _____
3 **A** I went to bed early.   _____
4 **A** I haven't been to China.   _____
5 **A** I don't have any children.   _____
6 **A** I can speak three languages.   _____
7 **A** I always have breakfast.   _____

9A past perfect

+		−	
I You He She **'d seen** the film before. It We They		I You He She **hadn't seen** the film before. It We They	
contractions: I'd = I had **I hadn't = I had not**			

?		✔		✘	
Had	I you he she **seen** it before? we they	**Yes,**	I you he she **had.** we they	**No**	I you he she **hadn't.** we they

Suddenly he remembered that he had seen the film before.

- Use the past perfect when you are already talking about the past, and want to talk about an earlier past action.
  When I woke up the garden was all white.
  It had snowed in the night.

  I arrived at the coffee bar twenty minutes late and my friends had already gone.
- Make the past perfect with *had / hadn't* + the past participle.
- The past perfect is the same for all persons.

> ⚠ Be careful: *I'd* can be *I had* or *I would*.

9B reported (or indirect) speech

reported sentences

Direct speech	Reported speech
'I love you.'	He said (that) he loved her.
'I want to see you again.'	He told her (that) he wanted to see her again.

- Use reported speech to say what another person said.

  I **love** you. ⤷ He said (that) he **loved** her.

- Other tenses change like this:

Direct speech	Reported speech
'I **can** help you.'	He said (that) he **could** help me.
'I'll phone you.'	He told me (that) he **would** phone me.
'I **met** a girl.'	He told me (that) he **had met** a girl.
'I've broken my leg.'	He said (that) **he had broken** his leg.

- *that* is optional after *say* and *tell*.
- Pronouns also change in reported speech, for example *I* changes to *he / she*, etc.

  I'm coming. ⤷ She told me that **she** was coming.

> ⚠ You can use *said* or *told* in reported speech but they are used differently.
> – You can't use *said* with an object or pronoun
>   NOT He said her he loved her
> – You must use *told* with an object,
>   *He told her that he loved her* NOT he told that…

reported questions

Direct speech	Reported speech
'Do you want to dance?'	He asked her **if she wanted** to dance.
'Where do you live?'	He asked her **where she lived**.

- In reported questions:
  – the tenses change in exactly the same way as in sentences, eg present to past, etc.
  – we don't use *do / did*.

  What **do** you **want?** ⤷

  *He asked me **what I wanted**.*

  NOT He asked me what did I want.

  – if the question begins with *do, can*, etc. add *if*.

  Do you like the music? ⤷ *He asked her **if** she liked the music.*

  Can you sing? ⤷ *She asked him **if** he could sing.*

  – the word order is subject + verb.

  Are you a student? ⤷ *He asked her if **she was** a student.*

  Have you seen the film? ⤷ *She asked him if **he had seen** the film.*

9A

a Match the sentence halves.

I couldn't get into my flat because	D	A	He had made other plans.
1 When our friends arrived		B	I realized that I'd seen it before.
2 I took the sweater back because		C	it was the first time she had flown.
3 Jack didn't come with us.		D	I'd forgotten my keys.
4 I turned on the TV		E	I hadn't turned off the cooker.
5 Jenny was nervous because		F	he had bought me the wrong size.
6 When the film started		G	we hadn't finished cooking the dinner.
7 At work I suddenly remembered that		H	to see what had happened.

b Complete the sentences. Put the verbs in the past simple or past perfect.

We ___*didn't get*___ a table in the restaurant because we ___*hadn't booked*___. (not get, not book)

1 I _____ Maria because she _____ her hair. (not recognize, cut)
2 My friend _____ to tell me I _____ my jacket in the car. (phone, leave)
3 When I _____ the TV, the match _____. (turn on, finish)
4 She _____ me the book because she _____ it yet. (not lend, finish)
5 He _____ all his exams because he _____ at all. (fail, not study)
6 When we _____ home we saw that somebody _____ the kitchen window. (get, break)

9B

a Write the sentences in reported speech.

He said, 'I love you.'   He told her that ___*he loved her*___.

1 'I'm tired.'   She said that she _____.

2 'I don't like rock music.'   He told her he _____.

3 'I'll book a table.'   He said _____.

4 'I've bought a new car.'   Paul told us that _____.

5 'I live in the city centre.'   She said that she _____.

6 'We can do it.'   They said that _____.

7 'I saw the film on TV.'   Julie said that _____.

b Make reported questions.

Do you want to dance?   He asked her if she ___*wanted to dance*___.

1 'Do you like football?'   Mike asked me if I _____.

2 'What music do you like?'   I asked her what music _____.

3 'Are you tired?'   She asked me _____.

4 'Have you been to New York?'   I asked them _____.

5 'Where did you live before?'   He asked me _____.

6 'Can you swim?'   She asked him _____.

7 'Where are you from?'   I asked him _____.

2 Prepositions of movement

Match the prepositions and pictures.

- [ ]   <u>un</u>der (the railway line)
- [ ]   a<u>long</u> (the street)
- [ ]   round / around (the lake)
- [ ]   <u>through</u> /θruː/ (the tunnel)
- [ ]   <u>in</u>to (the shop)
- [ ]   a<u>cross</u> (the road)
- [ ]   <u>o</u>ver (the bridge)
- [ ]   up (the steps)
- [ ]   past (the church)
- [ ]   <u>towards</u> /təˈwɔːdz/ (the lake)
- [*1*]   down (the steps)
- [ ]   out of (the shop)

b Cover the prepositions. Where did the dog go? *It went down the steps…*

⟳ **p.58**

Verbs

2 Confusing verbs

a Match the verbs and pictures.

wear	**carry**
clothes	a bag
win	**earn**
a prize	a salary
a match	
know	**meet**
somebody	somebody for the
something	first time
make	**do**
a cake	an exam, test, course
lunch, dinner	housework, the washing up
a noise	sport, yoga, aerobics
hope	**wait**
that something	for a bus
good will happen	
watch	**look at**
TV	a photo
look	**look like**
happy	your mother

⬅ **p.64**

b Cover the words and phrases and look at the pictures.
Test yourself or a partner.

Animals

a Match the animals and the pictures.

insects
- [ ] bee
- [ ] butterfly
- [ ] fly
- [ ] mosquito
- [ ] spider
- [18] wasp /wɒsp/

farm animals
- [ ] bull
- [ ] chicken
- [ ] cow /kaʊ/
- [ ] goat /ɡəʊt/
- [ ] horse
- [ ] pig
- [ ] sheep

wild animals
- [ ] bear
- [ ] camel
- [ ] crocodile
- [ ] dolphin
- [ ] elephant
- [ ] giraffe
- [ ] gorilla
- [ ] kangaroo
- [ ] lion
- [ ] mouse (plural *mice*)
- [ ] rabbit
- [ ] shark
- [ ] tiger
- [ ] whale

birds
- [ ] duck
- [ ] eagle
- [ ] swan /swɒn/

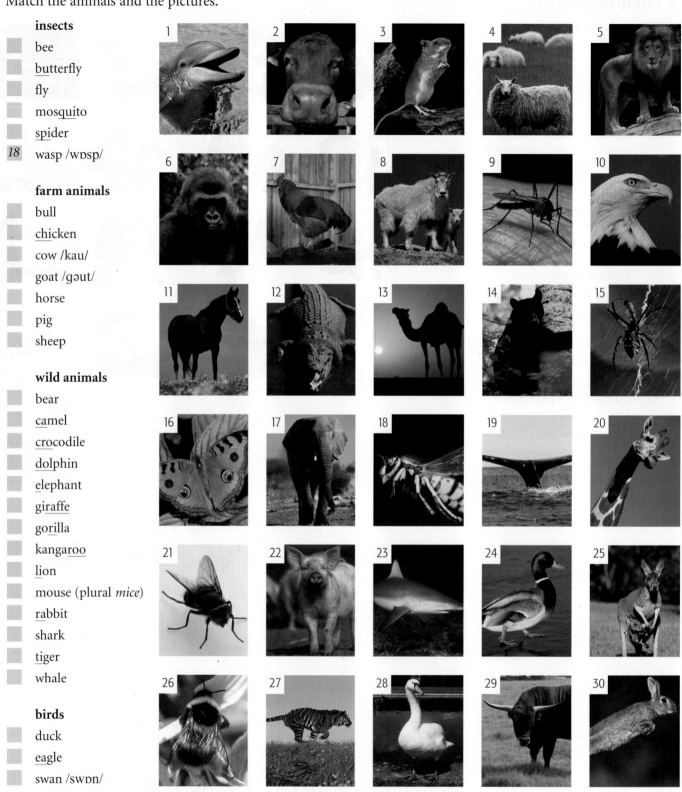

b Cover the words and look at the pictures. Test yourself or a partner.

⬅ p.67

a Match the phrases and the pictures.

get + adjective

▢	get di<u>v</u>orced
1	get <u>a</u>ngry
▢	get fit
▢	get <u>m</u>arried
▢	get lost

get + comparative

▢	get <u>o</u>lder
▢	get worse
▢	get <u>b</u>etter

get = buy / obtain

▢	get a job
▢	get a <u>ti</u>cket
▢	get a flat
▢	get a <u>news</u>paper

get + preposition (phrasal verbs)

▢	get on (well) with
▢	get on (opposite *off*)
▢	get into (opposite *out of*)
▢	get up

get = arrive

▢	get to work
▢	get home
▢	get to school

get = receive

▢	get a <u>sa</u>lary
▢	get a <u>le</u>tter
▢	get a <u>p</u>resent
▢	get an <u>e</u>-mail

b Cover the words and look at the pictures. Test yourself or a partner.

◖ **p.71**

1
2
3
4

5
6
7
8

9
10
11
12

get

13
14
15
16

17
18
19
20

21
22

a Match the sentences and the pictures.

[ ] We often stay up late at the weekend.

[ ] The match will be over at about 5.30.

[ ] I don't get on with my father.

[ ] I need to give up smoking.

[ ] Please put away your clothes.

[ ] Don't throw away that letter!

[ ] Turn down the music! It's very loud.

[ ] Turn up the TV! I can't hear.

[*1*] He looked up the words in a dictionary.

[ ] Could you fill in this form?

[ ] I want to find out about hotels in Madrid.

[ ] Please pick up that towel.

b Cover the sentences and look at the pictures.
Remember the phrasal verbs.

c Look at these other phrasal verb from Files 1–7.
Can you remember what they mean?

get up	turn on (the TV)	
come back	turn off (the TV)	
go back	put on (clothes)	
hurry up	take off (clothes)	
go away	try on (clothes)	
go out	give back (something you've borrowed)	look after (a child)
come in	take back (something to a shop)	look for (something you've lost)
sit down	call back (later)	look forward to (the holidays)
stand up	pay back (money you've borrowed)	
run away	write down (the words)	

Green = no object. The verb and the particle (*on, up*, etc.) are **never separated**.

I get up at 7.30.

Blue = + object. The verb and the particle (*on, up*, etc.) are **never separated**.

Look for your keys. NOT ~~Look your keys for~~.

Red = + object. The verb and the particle (*on, up*, etc.) **can be separated**.

Turn the TV on. OR *Turn on the TV.*

◐ **p.92**

Verb forms

A Verbs + infinitive

decide to	We decided to go to France.
forget to	Don't forget to turn off all the lights.
help to	He helped her to start the car.
hope to	We hope to see you again soon.
learn to	I'm learning to drive.
need to	I need to go the bank. I don't have any money.
offer to	He offered to take me to the airport.
plan to	They're planning to get married soon.
pretend	He pretended to be ill, but he wasn't really.
promise to	He promised to pay me back.
*remember to	Remember to bring your dictionaries tomorrow.
start	She started to cry.
*try to	I'm trying to find a job, but it's very hard.
want to	I want to go home.
would like to	I'd like to buy a new car.

⬅ **p.53**

B Verbs + -ing

enjoy	I enjoy reading in bed.
finish	Have you finished getting dressed?
go on (=continue)	I have to go on working until 9 o'clock.
hate	I hate getting up early.
like	I like having lunch in the garden.
love	I love waking up on a sunny morning.
(don't) mind	I don't mind cooking. It's OK.
spend (time)	She spends hours talking on the phone.
*start	I started reading this book last week.
stop	Please stop talking.

⬅ **p.55**

⚠ *start* can be used with both the infinitive and verb + *-ing* with no real difference in meaning.
*It started **raining**.*
*It started to **rain**.*

start + *-ing* is more common when we talk about a habit or a longer activity.
*I started **working** here in 1998.*
*When did you start **playing** the piano?*

try and *remember* can also be used + *ing* but the meaning is different.
*Why don't you try **doing** yoga?* = experiment with something
*Do you remember **meeting** him last year?*
= remember something after it happened

After *make* and *let* use the infinitive without *to*.
*Singing makes me **feel** good.*
*My parents don't let me **go** out during the week.*

Verb forms

C Irregular verbs

Infinitive	Past simple	Past participle
be	was	been
become	became	become
begin	began	begun
break	broke	broken
bring	brought /brɔːt/	brought
build	built /bɪlt/	built
buy	bought /bɔːt/	bought
can	could /kʊd/	–
catch	caught /kɔːt/	caught
come	came	come
cost	cost	cost
choose	chose	chosen
cut	cut	cut
do	did	done /dʌn/
drink	drank	drunk
drive	drove	driven
eat	ate	eaten
fall	fell	fallen
feel	felt	felt
find	found	found
fly	flew /fluː/	flown /fləʊn/
forget	forgot	forgotten
get	got	got
give	gave	given
go	went	gone
grow	grew /gruː/	grown
have	had	had
hear	heard /hɜːd/	heard
hit	hit	hit
keep	kept	kept
know	knew /njuː/	known /nəʊn/
learn	learnt	learnt
leave	left	left
lend	lent	lent
let	let	let
lose	lost	lost

Infinitive	Past simple	Past participle
make	made	made
meet	met	met
pay	paid	paid
put	put /pʊt/	put
read	read /red/	read /red/
ring	rang	rung
run	ran	run
say	said /sed/	said
see	saw /sɔː/	seen
sell	sold	sold
send	sent	sent
sing	sang	sung
shut	shut	shut
sit	sat	sat
sleep	slept	slept
speak	spoke	spoken
spend	spent	spent
stand	stood /stʊd/	stood
steal	stole	stolen
swim	swam	swum
take	took /tʊk/	taken
teach	taught	taught
tell	told	told
think	thought /θɔːt/	thought
throw	threw /θru/	thrown /θrəʊn/
understand	understood	understood
wake	woke	woken
wear	wore	worn
win	won /wʌn/	won
write	wrote	written

Vowel sounds

short vowels
long vowels
diphthongs

1 fish /fɪʃ/	2 tree /triː/	3 cat /kæt/	4 car /kɑː/
5 clock /klɒk/	6 horse /hɔːs/	7 bull /bʊl/	8 boot /buːt/
9 computer /kəmˈpjuːtə/	10 bird /bɜːd/	11 egg /eg/	12 up /ʌp/
13 train /treɪn/	14 phone /fəʊn/	15 bike /baɪk/	16 owl /aʊl/
17 boy /bɔɪ/	18 ear /ɪə/	19 chair /tʃeə/	20 tourist /ˈtʊərɪst/

Study Link MultiROM www.oup.com/elt/englishfile/pre-intermediate

Sounds and spelling

	usual spelling	⚠ but also
fish	**i** thin lips history kiss if since	English women busy decide repeat gym
tree	**ee** feel teeth **ea** teach mean **e** she we	people machine key niece
cat	**a** hands hat back catch carry match	
car	**ar** far arms scarf **a** fast pass after	aunt laugh heart
clock	**o** top lost socks wrong hot box	what watch want because
horse	**or** boring more **al** walk ball **aw** awful saw	water four bought thought abroad towards
bull	**u** pull push **oo** foot book look room	would should woman
boot	**oo** school choose **u*** rude use **ew** new knew	do suit juice shoe lose through
bird	**er** person verb **ir** dirty shirt **ur** nurse turn	earn work world worse
computer	Many different spellings, always unstressed. f<u>ur</u>ther <u>ner</u>vous <u>a</u>rr<u>i</u>ve p<u>o</u>l<u>ite</u> inv<u>en</u>tor <u>a</u>gr<u>ee</u>	

* especially before consonant + **e**

	usual spelling	⚠ but also
egg	**e** spell lend smell send very red	friendly head sweater any said
up	**u** sunny mustn't funny run lucky cut	come does someone enough young touch
train	**a*** face wake **ai** brain fail **ay** away pay	break steak great eight they grey
phone	**o*** open hope won't so **oa** coat goal	snow throw although shoulders
bike	**i*** smile bite **y** shy why **igh** might sights	buy eyes heights
owl	**ou** trousers round mouth blouse **ow** towel down	
boy	**oi** coin noisy boiling **oy** toy enjoy	
ear	**eer** beer engineer **ere** here we're **ear** near fear	really idea serious
chair	**air** airport stairs fair hair **are** square careful	their there wear bear
tourist	A very unusual sound. Europe furious sure plural	
/i/	A sound between /ɪ/ and /iː/. Consonant + **y** at the end of words is pronounced /i/. happy angry thirsty	
/u/	An unusual sound. education usually situation	

Consonant sounds

voiced
unvoiced

21 parrot /ˈpærət/   22 bag /bæg/   23 key /kiː/   24 girl /gɜːl/

25 flower /ˈflaʊə/   26 vase /vɑːz/   27 tie /taɪ/   28 dog /dɒg/

29 snake /sneɪk/   30 zebra /ˈzebrə/   31 shower /ˈʃaʊə/   32 television /ˈtelɪvɪʒn/

33 thumb /θʌm/   34 mother /ˈmʌðə/   35 chess /tʃes/   36 jazz /dʒæz/

37 leg /leg/   38 right /raɪt/   39 witch /wɪtʃ/   40 yacht /jɒt/

41 monkey /ˈmʌŋki/   42 nose /nəʊz/   43 singer /ˈsɪŋə/   44 house /haʊs/

Study Link MultiROM www.oup.com/elt/englishfile/pre-intermediate

Sounds and spelling

	usual spelling		⚠ but also
parrot	**p** promise possible copy cap **pp** opposite appearance		
bag	**b** belt body probably job cab **bb** rabbit rubbish		
keys	**c** camping across **k** skirt kind **ck** neck kick		chemist's stomach
girl	**g** grow goat forget begin **gg** foggy bigger		
flower	**f** find afraid safe **ph** elephant nephew **ff** off different		enough laugh
vase	**v** video visit lovely invent over river		of
tie	**t** try tell start late **tt** better sitting		walked dressed
dog	**d** did dead hard told **dd** address middle		loved tired
snake	**s** stops faster **ss** miss message **ce/ci** place circle		science
zebra	**z** zoo lazy freezing **s** reason lose has toes		
shower	**sh** shut shoes wash finish **ti** patient information (+ vowel)		sugar sure machine
television	An unusual sound. revision decision confusion usually garage		

	usual spelling		⚠ but also
thumb	**th** thing throw healthy tooth maths both		
mother	**th** weather the clothes sunbathe that with		
chess	**ch** chicken child beach **tch** catch match **t (+ure)** picture future		
jazz	**j** jacket just journey enjoy **dge** bridge judge		generous teenager
leg	**l** little less plan incredible **ll** will silly		
right	**r** really rest practice trainers **rr** borrow married		written wrong
witch	**w** wet twins worried win **wh** why which whale		one once
yacht	**y** yet year young yoga **before u** useful uniform		
monkey	**m** mountain modern remember smell **mm** summer swimming		
nose	**n** need nephew none any **nn** funny dinner		knees knock
singer	**ng** tongue fingers along thing bring going		think thank
house	**h** hit hate ahead perhaps hard		who whose whole

Study Link MultiROM www.oup.com/elt/englishfile/pre-intermediate

159

Never give a party if you will be the most interesting person there.

Mickey Friedman, American author

Are you a party animal?

1 GRAMMAR uses of the infinitive (with *to*)

a Complete the sentences with *to* and a verb.

meet	relax	~~not have~~	not tell
not worry	take	close	

1 I've decided <u>*not to have*</u> a birthday party this year. We'll just go out for a meal.

2 Would you like _____ my fiancé?

3 Please, try _____ about me. I'll be OK.

4 Oh no. I think I forgot _____ the kitchen window.

5 He promised _____ anybody about her problem.

6 She needs _____ more – she looks really stressed.

7 My dad offered _____ me to the party.

b Write sentences using the adjective and the correct form of the verb.

1 important / be

It's <u>*important to be*</u> there early this evening.

2 careful / not drop

Be _____ those plates!

3 dangerous / swim

It's _____ in this river.

4 difficult / sleep

Do you ever find it _____ at night?

5 interesting / talk to

She's always very _____ at parties.

6 nice / see

Hello! How _____ you again.

7 easy / use

Digital cameras are _____ .

c Complete the sentences with *to* and a verb.

argue	learn	take	have	~~study~~
make	buy	meet		

1 He's going to the library <u>*to study*</u> .

2 I go to evening classes _____ Spanish.

3 They're phoning the theatre _____ tickets.

4 She went to the café _____ something to eat.

5 Are you doing that _____ me angry?

6 I bought some books _____ with me on holiday.

7 I didn't come here _____ with you.

8 He goes to parties _____ new people.

Study Link **Student's Book p.134** *Grammar Bank 5A*

2 VOCABULARY verbs + infinitive

Fourteen examples of the word *to* are missing from this text. Can you put them back?

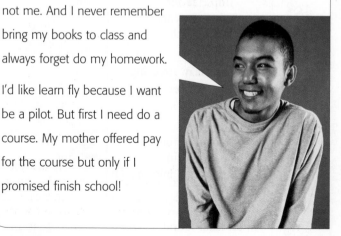

I'm Bill. I'm 16 and I've decided /leave school. I'm going
                                 ^to
leave next week. I'm hoping get a job with computers because I'm planning make lots of money.

I've tried work hard but I'm not a very good student. All the other students understand and learn do things quickly but not me. And I never remember bring my books to class and always forget do my homework.

I'd like learn fly because I want be a pilot. But first I need do a course. My mother offered pay for the course but only if I promised finish school!

Study Link **Student's Book p.154** *Vocabulary Bank*

3 PRONUNCIATION word stress

a Look at each pair of words. Which word is stressed on the second syllable? Under<u>line</u> the stress.

1 re<u>mem</u>ber   dangerous
2 promise   re<u>cep</u>tion
3 question   sur<u>vive</u>
4 decide   difficult
5 pre<u>tend</u>   birthday
6 offer   to<u>mor</u>row
7 airport   ad<u>vice</u>
8 children   es<u>cape</u>

b Practise saying the words.

4 READING

a Read the article and mark the sentences T (True) or F (False).

1 DJs are good for small parties.   _F_
2 A DJ is more expensive than live music.   ___
3 Some DJs need more space than others.   ___
4 A good DJ will only play music that he or she likes. ___
5 It's a good idea to ask how much space a DJ needs. ___
6 You need to pay more for an experienced DJ.   ___

b <u>Underline</u> five words you don't know. Use your dictionary to look up their meaning and pronunciation.

More Words to Learn

Write translations and try to remember the words.

Word	Pronunciation	Translation
cele<u>bra</u>tion *noun*	/selɪˈbreɪʃn/	
<u>hair</u>dresser *noun*	/ˈheədresə/	
<u>hair</u>style *noun*	/ˈheəstaɪl/	
psy<u>chi</u>atrist *noun*	/saɪˈkaɪətrɪst/	
<u>wed</u>ding re<u>cep</u>tion *noun*	/ˈwedɪŋ rɪˈsepʃn/	
im<u>per</u>sonal *adjective*	/ɪmˈpɜːsnəl/	
<u>mo</u>tivate *verb*	/ˈməʊtɪveɪt/	
rec<u>omm</u>end *verb*	/rekəˈmend/	
sur<u>vive</u> *verb*	/səˈvaɪv/	
in the <u>corn</u>er	/ɪn ðə ˈkɔːnə/	

QUESTION TIME

Can you answer these questions?

1 What do you want to do tonight?
2 What are you planning to do this weekend?
3 Is English easy or difficult to learn?
4 Which countries would you like to visit?
5 Do you think it's important to speak foreign languages?

Study Link MultiROM

Choosing a DJ

If you're having a big party for a wedding or an important birthday, then maybe you need a DJ. DJs are great if you don't have enough money or space to have a live band. A live band is more fun to watch, but a good DJ can be very entertaining and can keep people dancing all night.

Quality

If you decide to have a DJ, the most important thing to consider is quality. DJs need to be reliable, they need to have professional equipment, and they need to be experienced. And good DJs can be difficult to find.

Style of music

When you're hiring a DJ it's important to make sure that you like the music they play. If they're experienced, they should ask you what kind of party you're having, and what kind of people will be there. This information will help them to choose the music they play – and a good DJ always wants to entertain people.

Equipment

Different DJs can have very different amounts of equipment, from small CD and minidisc players to large sound systems and disco lighting, and even live dancers. It's important to ask how much equipment the DJ has so you can plan an appropriate space for him or her to work in. Again, a good DJ will be able to adapt his or her equipment to your needs.

Cost

When booking a DJ it's important to understand that you get what you pay for. Experienced DJs are in demand and ask for higher fees than newer, less experienced DJs. A good DJ means a great party, so try to spend as much as you can. And don't forget to enjoy yourself!

5 B What makes you feel good?

Happiness is when what you think, what you say, and what you do are all in harmony.

Mahatma Gandhi, Indian political leader

WORKBOOK

1 GRAMMAR verb + -ing

a Complete the sentences with the -ing form of the verbs in brackets.

1 I really hate ___tidying___ (tidy) my room!

2 I don't enjoy _____ (go) to the cinema on my own.

3 Will you please stop _____ (make) that noise!

4 We haven't finished _____ (eat) yet.

5 They'll go on _____ (talk) until you tell them to stop!

6 I love _____ (travel) to different places.

b Match the sentence beginnings and endings.

1 Do you ever dream of ☐ *c*

2 Are you interested in ☐

3 Please don't leave without ☐

4 Remember to say goodbye before ☐

5 We ended the evening by ☐

6 I'm really looking forward to ☐

a doing some part-time work?

b hearing about your holiday.

c stopping work and retiring? I do.

d thanking everybody for coming.

e saying goodbye to me.

f leaving tomorrow.

c Complete the text with the -ing form of these verbs.

drive	have	get	get up	go	imagine	leave	listen
read	~~send~~	stay	turn	take	~~write~~		

What makes you feel good?

Here are some more texts from our readers.

1 ¹ ___Writing___ and then ² ___sending___ a funny e-mail or text message to my friends. And of course, ³_____ their faces when they read it.

2 I really like ⁴_____ at night when there's no traffic, ⁵_____ to my favourite music. I feel completely free.

3 ⁶_____ in bed on Sunday morning and ⁷_____ the newspaper. Then ⁸_____ very late and ⁹_____ my dog for a long walk.

4 I enjoy ¹⁰_____ to the gym and really ¹¹_____ tired then ¹²_____ a long hot shower followed by a nice hot cup of tea. There's nothing better.

5 ¹³_____ off my computer at the end of the day, ¹⁴_____ work, and getting into my car to go home! It's the best moment of the day. I love it!

d Complete the text with the correct form of the verbs in brackets (-*ing* form or infinitive).

Getting out of the rat-race

More and more people are deciding ¹___to get___ (get) out of the rat-race. This means they want ²_____ (stop) ³_____ (work) in an office and move out of the city.

So, what are people doing instead of a 9–5 job? Well, many people hope ⁴_____ (set up) their own business. Perhaps they enjoy ⁵_____ (cook) for friends and have decided ⁶_____ (open) a café. Some people just want ⁷_____ (spend) time ⁸_____ (learn) something new.

Gill Yates and her husband, Tim, hated ⁹_____ (get up) every morning at 6 a.m. and ¹⁰_____ (catch) the train to London. They spent more hours ¹¹_____ (travel) than ¹²_____ (work)! They really liked ¹³_____ (sail) and ¹⁴_____ (surf), so they decided ¹⁵_____ (move) to Cornwall, in the south-west of England, and they started a business ¹⁶_____ (teach) other people to sail and surf. Gill says 'It's important to try ¹⁷_____ (be) happy with your life. You only get it once!'

Study Link Student's Book p.134 *Grammar Bank 5B*

2 PRONUNCIATION -*ing*

a Under<u>line</u> the stressed syllable in these words.

1 <u>sing</u>ing	4 listening	7 remembering
2 language	5 enjoying	8 pretending
3 morning	6 relaxing	

b Practise saying the words.

3 VOCABULARY verbs + -*ing*

Match the sentences.

1 She doesn't mind going if you can't. |c|
2 She loves going out. ☐
3 She hates gardening. ☐
4 She's stopped going to the gym. ☐
5 She's thinking of having a year off. ☐
6 She's started working again. ☐

a She doesn't do it any more.
b She's just begun.
c She's happy to do it.
d She really likes it.
e She hasn't decided yet.
f She really doesn't like it.

Study Link Student's Book p.154 *Vocabulary Bank*

More Words to Learn

Write translations and try to remember the words.

Word	Pronunciation	Translation
<u>fire</u> *noun*	/faɪə/	
<u>fo</u>rest *noun*	/ˈfɒrɪst/	
<u>my</u>stery *noun*	/ˈmɪstri/	
<u>na</u>ture *noun*	/ˈneɪtʃə/	
storm *noun*	/stɔːm/	
breathe *verb*	/briːð/	
con<u>trol</u> *verb*	/kənˈtrəʊl/	
(planes) take off *verb*	/teɪk ɒf/	
a whole day	/ə həʊl deɪ/	
it doesn't <u>matter</u>	/ɪt dʌznt ˈmætə/	

QUESTION TIME (?)

Can you answer these questions?

1 What do you enjoy doing when you're on holiday?
2 Do you think eating fish is healthier than eating meat?
3 Do you spend much time having breakfast?
4 Do you prefer eating out or cooking at home?
5 Are you good at remembering people's names?

Study Link MultiROM

5C How much can you learn in a month?

1 GRAMMAR *have to, don't have to, must, mustn't*

a Look at the pictures. Complete the sentences with the correct form of *have to*.

1 Chefs ___have to___ have clean hands to work with food.

2 Chefs _____ do the washing up.

3 A politician _____ be very old.

4 A politician _____ talk to lots of people.

5 Secretaries _____ know how to use computers.

6 Secretaries _____ be very tall.

7 _____ a pilot _____ be strong?

No, but they _____ be intelligent.

8 _____ a nurse _____ wear a uniform?

Yes, they usually _____ wear a blue or white dress.

b What do these signs mean? Write sentences with *must* or *mustn't*.

1 *You must fasten your safety belt.* fasten / safety belt

2 _____ stop / here

3 _____ smoke

4 _____ turn left

5 _____ wear / helmet

6 _____ walk / on the grass

c Complete the sentences with *mustn't* or *don't have to*.

1 I _don't have to_ wear a uniform to school.

2 You _____ smoke in a petrol station.

3 You _____ do the housework every day.

4 You _____ touch that wall. The paint's still wet.

5 You _____ climb up there – it's dangerous.

6 I _____ get up early at weekends.

Study Link **Student's Book p.134** *Grammar Bank 5C*

2 PRONUNCIATION silent letters

a Cross out the silent letters in these words.

1 mustn't	4 Wednesday	7 while
2 listen	5 knees	8 sign
3 half	6 know	9 walk

b Practise saying the words.

3 VOCABULARY modifiers

Order the words to make sentences.

1 British / American English / similar / very / are / and

   British and American English are very similar.

2 can / pronunciation / English / quite / difficult / be

   English _____.

3 Japanese / learning / isn't / easy / very

   Learning _____.

4 I / Hungarian / think / complicated / is / incredibly

   I _____.

5 is / bit / Czech / a / easier

   Czech _____.

6 Reading / is / vocabulary / a / to / way / really / useful / learn

   Reading _____.

4 READING

a Read the opinions about learning languages. Which do you think are the three best ideas?

WHAT'S THE BEST WAY TO …?

Learn a language

This week we ask students and teachers from all over the world for their ideas.

Péter, student, Hungary

Find something interesting to read in the language you're studying. Reading really helps you learn new vocabulary and grammar. I'm studying French, and I try to read a little French every day – you don't have to spend a long time doing it, maybe just five minutes looking at a French newspaper or website.

Ana, student, Spain

I think you have to concentrate on pronunciation from the beginning. You don't have to pronounce words perfectly, but you mustn't pronounce them in a way that people won't understand. I practise English pronunciation by repeating words after the tape or by saying the words in my head.

Elke, language teacher, Sweden

You have to listen to the language as much as you can. In Sweden a lot of people speak very good English, and I think it's partly because there are TV programmes in English, so you hear the language a lot.

Sompong, IT consultant, Thailand

I don't have a lot of time for studying, but I think that the Internet is an incredible resource for learners of English around the world. Everybody with a computer has access to millions of pages of English, and you don't have to leave home – in a few seconds you can find something interesting to read. You don't have to be studying to learn a language – you can be enjoying yourself.

Konrad, student, Poland

I think you have to have a good dictionary, it can really help you learn a language. It tells you what words mean, but it also gives you information about how words are used together, phrases, expressions, and pronunciation.

b Complete the sentences with the people's names.

1 ___Ana___ says that you don't need to have perfect pronunciation.

2 _____ and _____ think that having a computer will help you learn.

3 _____ thinks that a good reference book is important.

4 _____ thinks that if you hear a language, you'll get better at speaking it.

5 _____ says that reading can improve your vocabulary.

More Words to Learn

Write translations and try to remember the words.

Word	Pronunciation	Translation
experiment *noun*	/ɪkˈsperɪmənt/	
great-grandmother *noun*	/ɡreɪt ˈɡrænmʌðə/	
guide *noun*	/ɡaɪd/	
phrase book *noun*	/ˈfreɪzbʊk/	
complicated *adjective*	/ˈkɒmplɪkeɪtɪd/	
obligatory *adjective*	/əˈblɪɡətri/	
unbelievable/incredible *adjective*	/ʌnbɪˈliːvəbl/ /ɪnˈkredəbl/	
be good at *verb*	/biː ɡʊd æt/	
against (the rules) *preposition*	/əˈɡeɪnst/	
permitted	/pəˈmɪtɪd/	

Study idea

Think of personal examples to learn new words. What are you good at? What is against the rules in your school?

QUESTION TIME ?

Can you answer these questions?

1 Do you have to work or study at the weekend?
2 Do you have to get up early during the week?
3 Do you have to carry an identity card in your country?
4 Which side of the road do you have to drive on?
5 How old do you have to be to vote?

Study Link MultiROM

Some people believe football is a matter of life and death.
It is much more important than that.

Bill Shankly, Liverpool football manager

1 VOCABULARY sport, prepositions of movement

a Complete the puzzle.

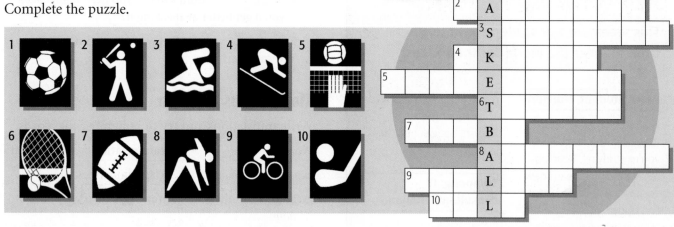

b Complete the sentences with the correct form of *play*, *do*, or *go*.

1 I _play_ rugby for a local team.

2 How often do you _____ swimming?

3 My father _____ golf every weekend.

4 We often _____ cycling at the weekend.

5 My sister _____ judo twice a week.

6 I can't _____ basketball because I'm too short!

c Read the definitions. Which of the sports in **a** are they?

1 In this sport you go <u>down</u> hills very quickly. You fix two long thin objects to your boots.   _skiing_

2 In this game there are two teams of nine players. Each player hits a ball with a bat, then runs round a circle.   _____

3 People who play this sport are usually very tall. They get points by throwing a ball through a net.   _____

4 You often play this sport indoors, but you can also play it on a beach. There are two teams. First you have to throw a ball over a high net, then use your hands to stop the ball hitting the ground on your side.   _____

5 You usually do this indoors, but you can also do it outdoors and even in the sea. You move your arms and legs to move through water.   _____

d <u>Underline</u> the prepositions of movement in **c**.

Study Link **Student's Book p.148** *Vocabulary Bank*

2 GRAMMAR expressing movement

a Look at the pictures and write sentences with these verbs and prepositions.

cycle   row   ~~run~~   go   get   ski   through   ~~across~~   out of   down   up   round

1 The dog *is running* _across_ the road.

2 The train _____ _____ the tunnel.

3 John _____ _____ the hill.

4 The men _____ _____ the mountain.

5 She _____ _____ the car.

6 They _____ _____ the lake.

b Look at the picture, read the story, and complete it with the prepositions.

across	into	out of	past	~~round~~	through
to	towards	under	along (x 2)		

Last day at school for boy with dirty shoes!

Last Wednesday started as normal for 15-year-old Michael Brewster at Hove Park School.

At 10.30 a.m., Michael's class were jogging ¹ _round_ the gym. But when Charles Duff, the sports teacher, told Michael to clean his dirty trainers, he got really angry. He ran ² _____ the gym, and back to the changing rooms where he found Mr Duff's keys. From there, he went ³ _____ the car park, got ⁴ _____ Mr Duff's Ford Mondeo and started the car. Then he drove ⁵ _____ the road, ⁶ _____ the bridge, ⁷ _____ the security guard and ⁸ _____ the school gates. Then he turned left and drove ⁹ _____ the road for about 100 metres ¹⁰ _____ the maths teacher's house. That was when he lost control. He tried to stop, went ¹¹ _____ the field and crashed into a tree. Michael has now left Hove Park School.

Study Link **Student's Book p.134** *Grammar Bank 5D*

3 PRONUNCIATION prepositions

Circle the preposition with a different sound.

![clock]	![computer]	![owl]
acr**o**ss	**a**long	**r**ound
al**o**ng	**o**ver	**u**nder
(**o**ver)	thr**ou**gh	d**ow**n
fr**o**m	t**o**wards	**ou**t

More Words to Learn

Write translations and try to remember the words.

Word	Pronunciation	Translation
fans *noun*	/fænz/	
goal *noun*	/gəʊl/	
hole *noun*	/həʊl/	
match *noun*	/mætʃ/	
net *noun*	/net/	
pitch *noun*	/pɪtʃ/	
player *noun*	/ˈpleɪə/	
stadium *noun*	/ˈsteɪdɪəm/	
track *noun*	/træk/	
score (a goal) *verb*	/skɔː/	

QUESTION TIME

Can you answer these questions?

1 What's your favourite sport? Why?
2 What was the last sporting event that you went to see?
3 How do you get from your English classroom to the nearest café?
4 When you go to class do you have to go over or under a bridge?
5 Do you go past a supermarket on your way home?

Study Link **MultiROM**

CAN YOU REMEMBER...? FILES 4&5

Complete each space with one word.

1 He's _____ to Paris three times.
2 Anna _____ arrived yet. I hope she's OK.
3 The Americans drive _____ slowly than the Italians.
4 He's the _____ intelligent boy in the school.
5 It's easy _____ meet people at a party.
6 I'm very lazy. I hate _____ exercise.
7 You _____ smoke in here. It's against the rules.
8 He drove _____ of the car park and into the street.

1 TAKING SOMETHING BACK

Complete the dialogue with one word in each space.

A Hi. How can I help you, madam?

B I ¹ b _ought_ these trousers yesterday and I've ² d_____ they're too big.

A Would you like to try a smaller size?

B No, thanks. I ³ t_____ on the small size yesterday and they were ⁴ t_____ small.

A Oh dear. Well, would you like to exchange them for something else?

B No, I'd prefer my money back. Could I have a ⁵ r_____, please?

A Of course. Do you have the receipt?

B Yes, ⁶ h_____ it is.

2 SOCIAL ENGLISH

Complete the dialogues.

1 **A** Wh _at_ did you th_____ of New York?

   B It was incredible.

2 **A** I didn't have enough time to see everything.

   B N_____ mind.

3 **A** What a l_____ evening!

   B Yes, it's beautiful, isn't it?

4 **A** What w_____ you l_____ to drink?

   B A coffee, please.

5 **A** Shall we go out for dinner?

   B What a g_____ i_____!

6 **A** Did you find the Post Office?

   B No, I got l_____.

3 READING

Union Square

Union Square is an important shopping area. Every major department store is nearby, and the square is also a centre for exclusive and high quality fashions, with names like Dior, Armani, Marc Jacobs, and Yves Saint Laurent all having boutiques in the area. If you like crowds, then Saturday afternoon would be the perfect time to visit. If you prefer to have the shops to yourself, then go when most of San Francisco is working. Weekday mornings are always quiet. Most stores are open until 8.00 p.m., and some even later. Here are some of our favourites.

BORDERS: Four floors of books, videos, DVDs, CDs, and more. There is a café on the second floor serving coffees and pastries, and a seating area overlooks Union Square. Special events, like author readings, are held on the third floor. 400 Post St., (415) 399-1633.

VIRGIN MEGASTORE: This huge three-storey music store offers one of the largest selections of CDs in San Francisco. Virgin also sells music books and videos and hosts the occasional artist album signing. The third floor café is popular. 2 Stockton St., (415) 397-4525.

BANANA REPUBLIC: You can find the latest fashions at prices that aren't cheap but won't break the bank. There are casual clothes that are still suitable for the office, like cashmere or lambswool sweaters. Accessories include hats, jackets, leather belts, and shoes. 256 Grant Ave., (415) 788-3087.

CAMPER: This Spanish-based company presents comfortable shoes in playful shapes and colours. The store itself is a 'work in progress', where customers can write or draw on the walls. 39 Grant Ave. (415) 296-1005.

a Read the text. Match the highlighted words to their meanings.

1 most recent _____ _latest_
2 small, expensive clothes shops _____
3 has a view over _____
4 won't be very expensive _____
5 lots of people _____
6 very big _____

b Where could you …?

1 buy a guide to the city _____ _Borders_
2 listen to a writer reading their new book _____
3 buy a new shirt _____
4 meet a music star _____
5 buy a new pair of boots _____
6 get a view over Union Square _____

If you want to find your prince, you will have to kiss a lot of frogs.

Anonymous

If something bad can happen, it will

1 GRAMMAR *if* + present, *will* + infinitive

a Match the sentence halves.

Here are six more examples of Murphy's Law:

1 If you don't remember to take
an umbrella, `c`

2 If you're in a hurry, ☐

3 If you lose something, ☐

4 If you forget to take a map, ☐

5 If a door says 'Pull', ☐

6 If you're looking for a partner, ☐

a something will go wrong to slow you down.

b you'll get lost.

c it'll rain.

d when you finally meet someone you like,
they won't like you.

e you'll push it first.

f you'll find it in the last place you look.

b Circle the correct form.

1 If you (take)/ will take Vitamin C, you won't
get a cold.

2 If the boys play football there, they **break /
will break** the window!

3 I'll call you tomorrow if I **hear / will hear**
any news.

4 If you **stay / will stay** in that hotel, it'll be
very expensive.

5 Jack **is / will be** sad if he doesn't see you
tomorrow.

6 If you **see / will see** an accident, call the
police!

7 You **get / 'll get** cold if you go out without
a coat.

8 If you go to bed early tonight, you **feel /
will feel** better in the morning.

c Read and match the texts to the correct pictures, A–G.

Traditions and Superstitions

A

B

C

D

E

F

G

1 The tooth fairy `D`

If a child ___*puts*___ (put) a lost tooth
under the pillow at night, the tooth fairy
_____ (come) during the night and
leave behind some money.

2 Good luck ☐

If the first butterfly you _____ (see)
in the year is white, you _____
(have) good luck all year.

3 Ladders ☐

If you _____ (walk) under a ladder,
you _____ (have) bad luck for a year.

4 Throwing a coin in a fountain ☐

If you _____ (throw) a coin into a
well or fountain and _____ (make) a
wish, the wish _____ (come) true.

5 Gold at the end of a rainbow ☐

If you _____ (dig) at the end of a
rainbow, you _____ (find) gold.

6 Mirrors ☐

If you _____ (break) a mirror, you
_____ (have) seven years bad luck.

7 Bees ☐

If a bee _____ (fly) into your home,
soon you _____ (have) a visitor. If
you _____ (kill) the bee, you
_____ (have) bad luck, or the visitor
_____ (be) someone you don't like.

d Complete the texts with the correct form of the verbs in
brackets.

Study Link **Student's Book p.136** *Grammar Bank 6A*

49

2 VOCABULARY confusing verbs

Complete the sentences with the correct verbs.

1 She was _wearing_ blue earrings and _carrying_ a red handbag. (carry, wear)

2 Tiger Woods has already _____ a lot of golf tournaments and _____ a fortune and he's still quite young. (earn, win)

3 **A** What did your mum _____?

  B She _____ me I couldn't go out tonight. (say, tell)

4 Jack was _____ that his girlfriend would call to say she was sorry. He _____ by the phone all evening but, unfortunately, she never called him. (hope, wait)

5 My parents _____ the whole wedding video but my brother decided to _____ the photos instead. (look at, watch)

6 I've _____ her for years. I _____ her when we were at university. (know, meet)

7 If you _____ the dinner, I'll _____ the washing up. (do, make)

8 **A** Do I _____ OK, Dad?

  B You _____ fantastic – in fact you _____ your mum when she was young. (look, look like)

> **Study Link** **Student's Book p.149** *Vocabulary Bank*

3 PRONUNCIATION long and short vowels

a Match each group of words to the correct sound.

1 Italy, fifty, spill   [b]

2 seat, he, sleep   ☐

3 was, long, shop   ☐

4 bored, door, your   ☐

5 look, took, push   ☐

6 do, supermarket, move   ☐

a   b   c

d   e   f

b Practise saying the words.

More Words to Learn

Write translations and try to remember the words.

Word	Pronunciation	Translation
law *noun*	/lɔː/	
queue *noun*	/kjuː/	
size *noun*	/saɪz/	
<u>sim</u>ple *adjective*	/ˈsɪmpl/	
in<u>ves</u>tigate *verb*	/ɪnˈvestɪgeɪt/	
kill *verb*	/kɪl/	
run a<u>way</u> *verb*	/rʌn əˈweɪ/	
spill *verb*	/spɪl/	
di<u>rect</u>ly *adverb*	/dɪˈrektli/	
to<u>geth</u>er *adverb*	/təˈgeðə/	

Study idea

Irregular verbs

1 When you learn new verbs, check in the dictionary to see if they are regular or irregular in the past tense.

2 If they are irregular, write IRR next to the verb in your vocabulary notebook, and write the past simple form next to it too.

3 Look up *investigate*, *kill*, *spill*, and *run* in your dictionary. Which one(s) is irregular? What's the past simple form?

QUESTION TIME

Can you answer these questions?

1 What will you do if it rains this weekend?

2 If you go to the cinema this weekend, what film will you see?

3 What will happen if you're late for your next English class?

4 If you leave home at 8.30 tomorrow morning, will you be late for work or school?

5 Will you pass your next English test if you don't study?

> **Study Link** **MultiROM**

> **Study Link** www.oup.com/elt/englishfile/pre-intermediate

All animals are equal – but some animals are more equal than others.
George Orwell, British writer

Never smile at a crocodile

1 GRAMMAR *if* + past, *would* + infinitive

a Complete the sentences with the correct form of the verbs in brackets.

1 If I ___*had*___ (have) a car, I *would drive* (drive) to work.

2 If I _____ (see) a tarantula, I _____ (be) terrified!

3 I _____ (not know) what to do if I _____ (find) a mouse in my kitchen.

4 What _____ you _____ (do) if you _____ (lose) your job?

5 If my sister _____ (be) older, she _____ (come) with me to the party.

6 My parents _____ (buy) a bigger house if they _____ (have) more money.

b Order the words to complete the sentences and questions.

1 I'd / shark / be / frightened / very
If I saw a _____ *shark, I'd be very frightened* _____.

2 saw / you / a / fire / if / do / you / would
What _____?

3 he / if / sailing / could / swim
He'd go _____.

4 new / lottery / clothes / won / she'd / lots of / the / buy
If she _____.

5 couldn't / if / would / do / they / people / watch / TV
What _____?

6 if / go / the / were / to / doctor's / I / you
I'd _____.

Study Link Student's Book p.136 *Grammar Bank 6B*

2 PRONUNCIATION word stress

a Write the words in the correct stress group.

afraid   animal   attack   chicken   crocodile   insect   mosquito   safari

1 Two syllables, stress on first syllable
<u>o</u>pen, _____, _____

2 Two syllables, stress on second syllable
a<u>bout</u>, _____, _____

3 Three syllables, stress on first syllable
<u>fi</u>nally, _____, _____

4 Three syllables, stress on second syllable
di<u>rec</u>tion, _____, _____

b Practise saying the words.

3 VOCABULARY animals

Complete the crossword.

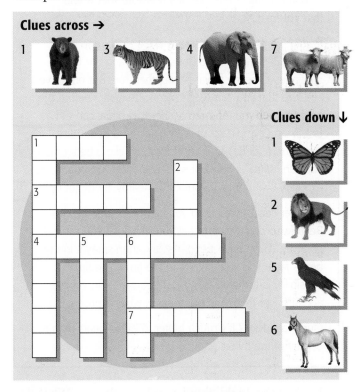

Study Link Student's Book p.151 *Vocabulary Bank*

4 READING

a Read the first part of the text and tick (✓) the things *you* would do.

Bear attack!

If you were hiking in the North American wilderness and you saw a bear coming slowly towards you, what would you do?

'I'd talk to it quietly.' ☐   'I'd climb a tree.' ☐

'I'd walk away slowly.' ☐   'I'd pretend to be dead.' ☐

'I'd try not to look at it.' ☐   'I'd spray pepper in its eyes.' ☐

'I'd make a loud noise.' ☐   'I'd try to fight it.' ☐

'I'd run.' ☐

b Now read the rest of the article. Which sentence is the best summary?

1 There's nothing you can do if a bear attacks you.

2 There are lots of things you can do if a bear attacks you.

3 Bears always try to avoid people.

Well, all of these are possible – the best thing to do depends on the mood that the bear is in. If it comes towards you slowly, experts say you should talk to it quietly, walk away as slowly as possible, and don't look the bear in the eye. It's possible that it will lose interest.

If not … then be aggressive, make a noise, and wave your hands. If this doesn't work, and the bear continues to come towards you, then run. But only if you are sure that you can reach somewhere safe before the bear reaches you. And remember that bears can run as fast as an Olympic sprinter. Don't climb a tree. Bears climb them all day long, and they can climb better than you can. Water is also not safe. Bears love water and are excellent swimmers. If your car is nearby, try to get inside.

If a bear attacks you, then you can pretend to be dead. Bears who don't want to eat you may lose interest and go away. If you have pepper spray, then spray it in the bear's face. This works 75% of the time. The final possibility is to fight back. Most bears are much bigger and stronger than you, but they may be surprised.

Our final advice? It's much better to avoid bears than to do any of the things above …

c Look at the highlighted words or phrases. What do you think they mean? Check with your dictionary.

More Words to Learn

Write translations and try to remember the words.

Word	Pronunciation	Translation
(river) bank *noun*	/bæŋk/	
fur coat *noun*	/fɜː kəʊt/	
pet *noun*	/pet/	
bark *verb*	/bɑːk/	
climb (a tree) *verb*	/klaɪm/	
disappear *verb*	/dɪsəˈpɪə/	
drown *verb*	/draʊn/	
lie on (the ground) *verb*	/laɪ ɒn/	
wave (your arms) *verb*	/weɪv/	
weigh *verb*	/weɪ/	

QUESTION TIME

Can you answer these questions?

1 Where would you go on holiday if you could go anywhere?

2 What would you do if you won the lottery?

3 What would your family think if you decided to live abroad?

4 What would you do if you saw a fire?

5 What would you do if you lost your mobile?

Study Link MultiROM

6C

Decisions, decisions

The first step to getting what you want out of life is this: Decide what you want.

Ben Stein, American writer

1 GRAMMAR may / might

a Mary is 18 and in her final year at school. She's thinking about her future. Complete her thoughts with *might* and a verb from the box.

fail	~~go~~	get	have to	live	rent
share	continue	not want			

Next year I ¹ *might go* to university. Or I ²_____ a job so I can start saving to buy a flat. I ³_____ living at home with my family or I ⁴_____ a flat. I ⁵_____ on my own or I ⁶_____ the flat with my friend, Sue. Although she ⁷_____ to share with me!

Or I ⁸_____ my exams! Oh no! If that happens, I ⁹_____ stay at school for another year. Why's life so difficult? Maybe I should do a course in decision-making!

b Read the sentences. Circle the correct form of *may / might (not)*.

1 If the taxi doesn't come soon, we **might** / might not miss the train.

2 I'm really tired so I **may** / **may not** go out tonight.

3 We love skiing so we **might** / **might not** go to the Alps for our next holiday.

4 Sue hasn't practised much so she **might** / **might not** fail her driving test.

5 I haven't seen Jim with Ella for a long time. They **may** / **may not** be together any more.

6 If you do lots of housework, your mum **might** / **might not** give you some money.

7 **A** I have a temperature and a headache.
   B Oh dear, you **might** / **might not** have a cold.

8 My parents **may** / **may not** come to the party – they think they'll be on holiday then.

Study Link **Student's Book p.136** *Grammar Bank 6C*

2 PRONUNCIATION word stress

a Under<u>line</u> the stressed syllable in these words.

1 organi<u>za</u>tion   5 imagination

2 invitation   6 translation

3 election   7 communication

4 information   8 decision

b Practise saying the words.

3 VOCABULARY noun formation

a Complete the chart with *-tion* or *-sion* nouns or the correct verb. Use your dictionary if necessary.

Verb	Noun
communicate	*communication*
conclude	conclusion
correct	_____
_____	confusion
demonstrate	_____
inject	_____
_____	organization
predict	_____

b Complete the sentences with verbs or nouns from a.

1 And finally, in ___*conclusion*___, I'd just like to thank you all very much for being here today.

2 E-mails and mobiles have made it much easier to _____.

3 I need to go to the doctor's for an _____.

4 The scientists gave an impressive _____ of the new robot.

5 Let me make a _____ about the future. I don't think there will be any more global wars.

6 Can you help me _____ the conference?

53

4 READING

Life in Y3K

Most of us don't know what life will be like in the future, or even where we'll be a year from now, but it's fun to speculate. So, what might the world be like in the year 3000 (or Y3K as it's now called)? Here's what one expert suggests:

Q **What forms will our bodies have in Y3K?**

A We will be bigger and we'll need more food. The average adult male might weigh about 100 kilos. People will live for hundreds of years, and will have computers in their brains.

Q **Computers in their brains! What do you mean?**

A We will soon be able to repair the human brain, and finally replace it completely. In the future you might be able to record all your experiences on a disk, so you can re-live them when you want to. Communication will be 100 times faster too. Now we communicate by speaking, but in the future we may communicate by thoughts and images.

Q **Will we still die?**

A We might be able to avoid death, replacing all our body parts when we need to. If you die, it may only be by choice. It could be your choice – or it might be the choice of the government that runs your mind computer.

Q **And what will humans do with their time?**

A Computers will do all the work. All manufacturing production will be automated. We might just enjoy ourselves while technology does everything.

Q **What about space travel?**

A We might take control of space and live there too. There might be colonies on Mars or on other planets. Robots will travel far into the galaxy and we may find alien life.

Q **But will we be happier?**

A Well, I'm an optimist. I think in the end most of us will be happy and the world will be a better place. But who knows?

---

a Read the interview. Mark the sentences T (True) or F (False).

1 People will be larger and live much longer in the future. _T_

2 We won't be able to replace our brains. ___

3 We might be able to communicate without speaking. ___

4 We will definitely not die. ___

5 We won't need to work. ___

6 People and robots will travel in space. ___

7 We won't find any aliens. ___

8 The expert thinks the world may be a better, happier place in the future. ___

b Underline five words you don't know. Use your dictionary to look up their meaning and pronunciation.

More Words to Learn

Write translations and try to remember the words.

Word	Pronunciation	Translation
options *noun*	/ˈɒpʃnz/	
(in)decisive *adjective*	/dɪˈsaɪsɪv/	
ask for (advice) *verb*	/ɑːsk fɔː/	
belong *verb*	/bɪˈlɒŋ/	
change your mind *verb*	/tʃeɪndʒ jə maɪnd/	
compare *verb*	/kəmˈpeə/	
confuse *verb*	/kənˈfjuːz/	
make a decision *verb*	/meɪk ə dɪˈsɪʒn/	
make a list *verb*	/meɪk ə lɪst/	
take your time *verb*	/teɪk jə taɪm/	

QUESTION TIME ?

Can you answer these questions with *may* or *might*?

1 What are you going to do tonight?

2 What are you going to wear tomorrow?

3 What are you going to have for dinner tomorrow?

4 What do you think you'll do next weekend?

5 What's the next thing you're going to buy?

Study Link MultiROM

I owe my success to having listened respectfully to the very best advice,
and then going away and doing the exact opposite.

G. K. Chesterton, British writer

What should I do?

1 GRAMMAR *should / shouldn't*

a Match the sentences to the pictures. Complete them with *should* or *shouldn't*.

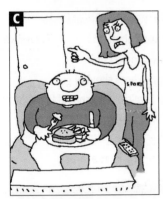

1 He ___should___ have a haircut. ☐B

2 She _____ buy a new sweater. ☐

3 He _____ drink coffee all day. ☐

4 'You _____ smoke, it's very bad for you.' ☐

5 She _____ drive when she's tired. ☐

6 'You _____ do more exercise.' ☐

b Read the problems. Complete the advice with *should / shouldn't* and a verb from the box.

> **A** I love going out at night and then watching TV when I get home. The trouble is, I'm always tired at work the next day. What should I do?
>
> **B** I have a bad pain in my neck. When I move my head, it gets much worse. What is your advice?
>
> **C** There is a really nice shirt on sale in my local shop. It's expensive, but I can just afford it. Should I buy it?
>
> **D** My colleague earns more money than I do, but does half the amount of work. It's really making me angry. What should I do?
>
> **E** My children are six and nine years old. They love to watch horror films, but when they do they can't sleep at night. Any advice?
>
> **F** I hate waiting in queues. After about two minutes I get really angry and want to hit someone. Please help.
>
> **G** I'm 23 and lonely. I work from home and I never get a chance to meet anybody. What should I do?

be   go (x2)   ~~tell~~   watch   buy   join

1 You ___should tell___ your boss. He might offer you more money. ☐D

2 You _____ so impatient. Try to relax more. ☐

3 You _____ to bed so late! ☐

4 You _____ to the doctor's immediately. ☐

5 You _____ it before someone else does. ☐

6 You _____ a dating agency. ☐

7 They _____ horror movies at that age! ☐

c Match the advice to the problems in **b**.

Study Link **Student's Book p.136** *Grammar Bank 6D*

2 PRONUNCIATION /ʊ/

a Circle the word in each group which has the /ʊ/ sound.

1 lock (would) so not

2 problem worth out should

3 could women company stop

4 touch borrow understood worth

5 good come soon argue

b Practise saying the words.

3 VOCABULARY *get*

Complete the sentences with the correct form of *get* and one of these words.

---
angry e-mails home married taller
tickets on ~~worse~~ off lost
---

1 **A** The pain in my back's ___getting___ ___worse___.

   B You should go to the doctor's.

2 I _____ 25 _____ from my boss yesterday. I spent all day answering them.

3 You shouldn't _____ _____ with him for breaking the window. He's only three!

4 **A** Can you _____ me two _____ for Friday's concert?

   B I might be able to.

5 My mum and I are great friends but I don't _____ _____ with my father very well.

6 John usually finishes work very late. When he _____ _____ his children are always in bed.

7 At what age do you think young people should _____ _____?

8 My granddaughter _____ _____. She's growing very fast.

9 Would you like my seat? I _____ _____ the bus at the next stop.

10 I didn't have a map so I _____ _____.

Study Link **Student's Book p.152** *Vocabulary Bank*

More Words to Learn

Write translations and try to remember the words.

Word	Pronunciation	Translation
<u>cup</u>board *noun*	/ˈkʌbəd/	
sug<u>ges</u>tion *noun*	/səˈdʒestʃn/	
(good) taste *noun*	/teɪst/	
<u>des</u>perate *adjective*	/ˈdespərət/	
of<u>fen</u>ded *adjective*	/əˈfendɪd/	
<u>sen</u>sitive *adjective*	/ˈsensətɪv/	
lock *verb*	/lɒk/	
make an ex<u>cuse</u> *verb*	/meɪk ən ɪkˈskjuːs/	
treat *verb*	/triːt/	
it's not worth it	/ɪts nɒt wɜːθ ɪt/	

CAN YOU REMEMBER...? FILES 5&6

Complete each space with one word.

1 I went to the shop _____ buy a paper.

2 I love _____ breakfast in bed on Sundays.

3 I _____ have to work tomorrow. It's my day off.

4 The man ran _____ the tunnel and then across the road.

5 If we don't hurry, we _____ catch the 6 o'clock train.

6 What _____ you do if you saw a snake?

7 My sister _____ come this weekend, but I'm not sure.

8 I think you _____ do some exercise. You aren't very fit.

Study Link www.oup.com/elt/englishfile/pre-intermediate

1 ASKING FOR MEDICINE

Complete the dialogue with these words.

take   hurts   much   might   are
have   ~~help~~   often   times   think

A Good afternoon. How can I ¹___*help*___?

B I have a headache and my back ²_____ as well.

A Do you ³_____ a temperature?

B Yes, I think I do a bit.

A ⁴_____ you allergic to anything?

B No, I don't ⁵_____ so.

A OK, it sounds as if you ⁶_____ have flu, or a bad cold.

B Do you have anything I can ⁷_____?

A Yes, try these. You take one three ⁸_____ a day.

B Sorry, how ⁹_____?

A Three times a day.

B Great. How ¹⁰_____ are they?

A They're €6.75 for 24.

2 SOCIAL ENGLISH

Complete the dialogues.

1 **A** B___*less*___ you! Are you OK?

   B Yes, I'm fine. I have a cold, that's all.

2 **A** H_____ about going somewhere for a drink?

   B That s_____ fantastic. Where s_____ we go?

   A I don't m_____. You c_____.

3 **A** I'm really s_____ I missed that film on TV.

   B Yes, it's a p_____. It was really good.

3 READING

a Match the signs to their meaning.

1 Keep out of reach of children

2 Do not exceed the stated dose ✗

3 [no mobile phones]

4 Watch out! Pickpockets operating in this area

5 [no smoking]

6 Mind the step

7 Vehicles & contents left entirely at owners' risk

8 [no tap water]

9 FIRE DOOR Keep closed at all times

10 Slow! Dangerous crossroads

11 Please wait here to be seated

12 [no radios]

[2] You should be careful not to take too much of this medicine.

☐ You have to wait until a waiter shows you where to sit.

☐ You must keep this medicine somewhere safe.

☐ You mustn't smoke here.

☐ You shouldn't leave anything valuable in your car.

☐ You should be careful or you might fall over.

☐ You mustn't drink this water.

☐ You must make sure that the door is never left open.

☐ You should be careful with your belongings.

☐ You have to turn your mobile off.

☐ You must drive carefully here.

☐ You mustn't use radios in this park.

b <u>Underline</u> five words or phrases you don't know. Use your dictionary to look up their meaning and pronunciation.

I am not afraid of death, I just don't want to be there when it happens.

Woody Allen, American film director

Famous fears and phobias

1 VOCABULARY phobias

Complete the sentences.

1 Another word for afraid is f *rightened* .

2 If you are very afraid you are t_____ .

3 Two insects which a lot of people are afraid of are

   w_____ and s_____ .

4 When some people are afraid, they p_____ .

5 If you suffer from claustrophobia, it means that

   you don't like being in c_____

   s_____ .

6 People who are afraid of h_____ don't like

   going up tall buildings.

2 GRAMMAR present perfect + *for* and *since*

a Circle the correct word, *for* or *since*, to
  complete each sentence.

  1 I've been afraid of spiders **for** / (**since**) I was ten.

  2 She's been afraid of flying **for** / **since** many years.

  3 I've had this watch **for** / **since** three months.

  4 We haven't been back there **for** / **since** the
    accident happened.

  5 **A** How long have you been here?

    B **For** / **Since** ten o'clock. I've been waiting
    for / **since** two hours.

  6 They haven't slept **for** / **since** the baby was born!

  7 He hasn't ridden a horse **for** / **since** he fell off
    one when he was twelve.

  8 **A** How long have you known your husband?

    B **For** / **Since** ages! We met when we were
    nineteen and have been together **for** / **since**
    then.

b Complete the text with *for* and *since*.

A photographer's life

Martha Schwarz, 29, freelance photographer

I've had three different homes [1] *since* I was born. My family and I lived in a small flat [2]_____ the first five years of my life, then we moved to a larger one after my second sister was born. My parents have lived there [3]_____ then, and don't want to move anywhere else because they love the area.

I moved out when I got engaged and I've lived in a small house near the Danube [4]_____ the last seven years. My husband and I have been married [5]_____ almost five years now and we're expecting our second child soon. We already have a daughter – it was her second birthday yesterday – and so we're hoping for a son this time. I've been pregnant [6]_____ February.

I've been a professional photographer [7]_____ nearly six years now and I love it. I worked for *Newsweek* [8]_____ four years and I've been freelance [9]_____ I left. I much prefer working for myself, although I miss all the fun of working in an office – and the gossip of course!

My favourite camera is my old Nikon 601. I've had it [10]_____ my 21st birthday. I must have taken about twenty thousand photos with it, and it still works perfectly!

c Complete the questions about Martha. Use *How long* or *When* and the verb in brackets.

1 *How long have* her parents _____*lived*_____ in the area? (live)

They've lived there since her sister was born.

2 _____ Martha _____? (move out)

When she got engaged.

3 _____ she and her husband _____ married? (be)

For almost five years.

4 _____ she _____ pregnant? (be)

Since February.

5 _____ she _____ a professional photographer? (become)

Nearly six years ago.

6 _____ she _____ freelance? (be)

Since she left *Newsweek*.

7 _____ she _____ her Nikon 601? (get)

She got it for her 21st birthday.

d Correct the mistake in each sentence.

1 Gill lives here for seven years.

Gill has lived here for seven years.

2 How long is she a professional dancer?

_____?

3 They were married since 2000.

_____.

4 He has been in France for February.

_____.

5 How long do you have your car?

_____?

6 He's had this job since eight years.

_____.

7 She has three homes since she was born.

_____.

8 My parents live in the same house for many years.

_____.

Study Link Student's Book p.138 *Grammar Bank 7A*

3 PRONUNCIATION /ɪ/ and /aɪ/

a Circle the correct sound for each pair of words.

1	dish, live (v)	(/ɪ/)	/aɪ/
2	since, this	/ɪ/	/aɪ/
3	fly, frightened	/ɪ/	/aɪ/
4	time, spider	/ɪ/	/aɪ/
5	child, wine	/ɪ/	/aɪ/
6	miss, silly	/ɪ/	/aɪ/
7	high, heights	/ɪ/	/aɪ/
8	six, film	/ɪ/	/aɪ/

b Practise saying the words.

More Words to Learn

Write translations and try to remember the words.

Word	Pronunciation	Translation
bomb *noun*	/bɒm/	
boat *noun*	/bəʊt/	
scene *noun*	/siːn/	
treatment *noun*	/ˈtriːtmənt/	
giant *adjective*	/ˈdʒaɪənt/	
hairy *adjective*	/ˈheəri/	
affect *verb*	/əˈfekt/	
fight *verb* (past = fought)	/faɪt/	
in this respect	/ɪn ðɪs rɪˈspekt/	
the rest (of us)	/ðə rest/	

QUESTION TIME

Can you answer these questions?

1 How long have you known your oldest friend?
2 How long have you had your mobile phone?
3 How long have you studied English?
4 How long have you had your shoes?
5 How long have you been in your English class?

Study Link MultiROM

7B **Born to direct**

In films the director is God; in documentaries God is the director.

Alfred Hitchcock, British film director

WORKBOOK

1 VOCABULARY life events

Complete the phrases.

1 I was   `c`
2 I went   ☐
3 I left   ☐
4 I started   ☐
5 I fell   ☐
6 We got   ☐
7 We had   ☐
8 I retired   ☐

a on my 60th birthday.
b in love with Ana at university.
c born in 1940.
d to school when I was five.
e work when I was 21.
f two children.
g school when I was 18.
h married in 1962.

2 PRONUNCIATION word stress

a Write the words in the correct group.

~~successful~~	career	appear
famous	cinema	direct	director
violence	ticket	actor

Stress on 2nd syllable	Stress on 1st syllable
successful	

b Practise saying the words.

3 GRAMMAR present perfect or past simple?

a Circle the correct verb forms.

I ¹ **knew** / (**'ve known**) Teresa for ages, almost since we ² **were** / **'ve been** born. We ³ **met** / **'ve met** at the same nursery school when we ⁴ **were** / **'ve been** only four years old and we ⁵ **'re** / **'ve been** friends since then. We ⁶ **went** / **'ve been** to the same primary school, we ⁷ **were** / **have been** in the same class at secondary school, and now we're at the same university.

    At least we don't study the same subjects. She's doing Geography and I ⁸ **chose** / **have chosen** History. But I've always wanted to be a teacher, and yesterday Teresa ⁹ **told** / **'s told** me that she wants to do the same thing!

    We ¹⁰ **'ve been** / **were** together for a long time, and we ¹¹ **shared** / **'ve shared** a lot of great experiences – maybe teaching together will be next!

Cathy Thomson   Teresa Marsh

b Write the verbs in the past simple or present perfect. Use contractions where necessary.

1 **A** How long ____*have*____ you ____*lived*____ in Washington? (live)
   B Since last November.

2 **A** I _____ divorced last year. (get)
   B How long _____ you married? (be)

3 I _____ university when I was 22, and since then I _____ as a civil engineer. (leave, work)

4 **A** Where _____ you _____ for your last holiday? (go)
   B We _____ the Orient Express to Venice. (take)

5 **A** How long _____ you _____ that car? (have)
   B A long time! I _____ it in 1994. (buy)

6 I _____ Emma since she _____ to Australia three years ago. (not see, move)

Study Link **Student's Book p.138** *Grammar Bank 7B*

4 READING

Hayao Miyazaki

1 The Japanese film director Hayao Miyazaki is one of the greatest animators in modern cinema. Films like *Heidi,* and *Marco, 3000 miles in search of mother* have made him famous all over the world.

☐ In1971 Miyazaki left Toei Douga Animation and worked with several other companies He made *Heidi,* and *Marco, 3000 miles in search of mother* which were shown as TV series all over the world.

☐ In 1952 they moved back to Tokyo. When Hayao was at secondary school he saw his first cartoon film, *The Legend of the White Snake.* He fell in love with the heroine, Pai-nyan and cried all night. It was this film which started his interest in animation.

☐ In 1985 he and his friend and colleague Takahata started a film studio called Studio Ghibli. Since then Miyazaki has directed, written, and produced many other films with Takahata. All of these films have been major successes, particularly *Princess Mononoke* and the recent *Spirited Away.*

☐ But he still loved cartoons. After he left university in 1963 he started work at Toei Douga Animation and he became very successful. While he was working there he met another artist, Akemi Ota. They got married in 1965 and they have two sons. They live in Tokyo.

☐ But when he tried to draw he found he could only draw planes not people. So when he left school he decided to study economics and political science at university.

☐ Hayao Miyazaki was born in Tokyo on January 5, 1941. His family had a company which made parts for planes, and when he was young Hayao spent a lot of time drawing planes. After the war, the family moved to Utsunomiya City.

a Read the text about Miyazaki. Order the paragraphs 1–7.

b Circle the correct verb form in the questions.

1 When (was) / has been Hayao Miyazaki born?

2 When **did his family move** / **have his family moved** back to Tokyo?

3 When **did he see** / **has he seen** his first cartoon film?

4 How long **did he work** / **has he worked** for Toei Douga Animation?

5 How long **was he married** / **has he been married**?

c Read the text again and answer the questions in **b**.

More Words to Learn

Write translations and try to remember the words.

Word	Pronunciation	Translation
career *noun*	/kəˈrɪə/	
drugs *noun*	/drʌgz/	
entrance *noun*	/ˈentrəns/	
episode *noun*	/ˈepɪsəʊd/	
parking ticket *noun*	/ˈpɑːkɪŋ ˈtɪkɪt/	
prison *noun*	/ˈprɪzn/	
role *noun*	/rəʊl/	
violence *noun*	/ˈvaɪələns/	
nominate *verb*	/ˈnɒmɪneɪt/	
play (the part of) *verb*	/pleɪ/	

QUESTION TIME ?

Can you answer these questions?

1 When did you start school?

2 Where did you go to primary school?

3 How long have you lived in this town?

4 How old were you when you went to secondary school?

5 How many times have you been abroad?

Study Link MultiROM

7 C I used to be a rebel

1 GRAMMAR *used to*

a Complete the sentences with the correct form of *used to* and the verb in brackets.

1 *Did you use to enjoy* (you / enjoy) maths at school?

2 I _____ (not like) flying, but I love it now.

3 We _____ (be) friends, but we don't get on now.

4 _____ (Colin / work) for IBM before he came here?

5 Summers _____ (not be) as hot as they are now.

6 She _____ (live) with her mother, but now she lives with her father.

7 I _____ (not do) any exercise.

8 _____ (he / play) for Manchester United?

b Correct the mistakes in the highlighted phrases.

1 I use to go to the cinema more often.   *used*

2 He used wear a uniform when he was at school.   _____

3 We didn't used to understand our French teacher.   _____

4 Did you used to work in an office?   _____

5 She use to work late but now she finishes at 5.00.   _____

6 Did your children used go to school on Saturdays?   _____

Study Link **Student's Book p.138** *Grammar Bank 7C*

2 PRONUNCIATION consonants

a Circle the word with a different consonant sound.

years	science	school	teenager
rules	class	change	great
used to	friends	child	journalist

b Practise saying the words.

3 VOCABULARY school subjects

Match the school subjects and the sentences.

1 Foreign languages [c]

2 Geography ☐

3 History ☐

4 Literature ☐

5 Maths ☐

6 Physical education ☐

7 Science ☐

8 Technology ☐

a $23 \times 48 = 1,104$

b *Hamlet* is one of Shakespeare's greatest plays.

c How do you say 'Good morning' in French?

d Remember to click on the icon to select the program.

e Napoleon died in 1821.

f I want everyone to run round the track four times.

g What's the capital of Norway?

h A water molecule has one oxygen atom and two hydrogen atoms.

4 READING

a Read the interview. Write the questions in the correct place.

Did you have a favourite teacher?

~~Where did you go to school?~~

Did you ever get into trouble?

What's the most important lesson you've learned in life?

What did you want to do when you were young?

What subjects were you good at?

My schooldays

DANIELA NARDINI,
actor, star of the
BBC series *This Life*

interview by Leila Farrah

1 *Where did you go to school?*

St Mary's Primary School in Largs, a small Scottish town. Then Largs Academy, the local secondary school.

2 _____

No, my school reports usually used to say 'friendly and well-behaved'. I don't think I was rebellious, in fact I used to be quite shy. I became more of a rebel in secondary school. I stayed until I was eighteen, but I was quite lazy and uninterested and I didn't use to do very much work.

3 _____

I used to love English and art, but I wasn't very good at maths. In English lessons we used to read plays, and I sat at the back of the class thinking, 'Why can't you all act a bit better?' It was the first time I thought about being an actor.

4 _____

I used to love Miss O'Toole, one of my primary teachers. I loved her because at school, even if you were doing maths with her, which I didn't like, she used to let me draw, and she never got angry.

At secondary school I liked my biology teacher, Mr Scott, and my geography teacher, Mr Brunei, because they were nice people, although I wasn't very good at their subjects.

5 _____

As a little girl I wanted to be a movie star, and I used to make my dad act out scenes with me. I also wanted to be a make-up artist.

6 _____

Try to do the thing you love most – even if you think it's silly. I've learned most through working and acting, because it teaches me about life. To earn money by doing something you love can only make you a happier person.

b Mark the sentences T (True), F (False), or ? (Doesn't say).

1 Daniela went to school in Scotland.   *T*

2 She went to primary school with her brother.   ___

3 She worked hard at secondary school.   ___

4 Her secondary school was for boys and girls.   ___

5 The children in her class at secondary school weren't very good actors.   ___

6 Miss O'Toole used to get angry with her students.   ___

7 She didn't want to be an actor when she was very young.   ___

8 She thinks it's important to enjoy your job.   ___

More Words to Learn

Write translations and try to remember the words.

Word	Pronunciation	Translation
<u>dra</u>ma *noun*	/ˈdrɑːmə/	
<u>pro</u>test *noun*	/ˈprəʊtest/	
qualifi<u>ca</u>tions *noun*	/kwɒlɪfɪˈkeɪʃnz/	
<u>re</u>bel *noun*	/ˈrebl/	
bright (= intelligent) *adjective*	/braɪt/	
de<u>te</u>riorate *verb*	/dɪˈtɪəriəreɪt/	
es<u>pe</u>cially *adverb*	/ɪˈspeʃli/	
<u>re</u>cently *adverb*	/ˈriːsntli/	
ac<u>cord</u>ing to *preposition*	/əˈkɔːdɪŋ tʊ/	
at war	/ət wɔː/	

QUESTION TIME   ?

Can you answer these questions?

1 Who used to be your best friend at primary school?

2 What food did you use to like when you were a child?

3 Which books did you use to like when you were a child?

4 Do you watch more television now than you used to?

5 Do you do more exercise now than you used to?

Study Link MultiROM

7D The mothers of invention

WORKBOOK

1 GRAMMAR passive

a Order the words to make sentences.

1 relieve pain / used / is / Aspirin / to
   Aspirin is used to relieve pain.

2 named / The sandwich / after / was / the Earl of Sandwich

   _____

   _____ .

3 designed / Christopher Wren / St Paul's Cathedral / was / by

   _____

   _____ .

4 based / This film / a true story / is / on

   _____

   _____ .

5 published / The first crossword puzzle / in 1913 / was

   _____

   _____ .

6 the Diner's Club / issued / The first credit card / by / was

   _____

   _____ .

7 very often / not used / The fax machine / these days / is

   _____

   _____ .

8 discovered / was / by / Alexander Fleming / Penicillin

   _____

   _____ .

b Write sentences in the present or past passive.

1 President Kennedy / assassinate / 1963
   President Kennedy was assassinated in 1963.

2 Champagne / made / France
   Champagne is made in France.

3 What / your dog / call

   _____?

4 Television / invent / John Logie Baird

   _____ .

5 This room / clean / every morning

   _____ .

6 Her flat / design / a famous architect

   _____ .

7 Stamps / only sell / in the Post Office

   _____ .

8 Where / those shoes / make

   _____?

c Rewrite the sentences in the passive.

1 The police stopped me last night.
   I was stopped by the police last night.

2 Elton John sang *Crocodile Rock*.
   Crocodile Rock _____ .

3 My cousin took all the photographs at our wedding.
   All the photographs _____

4 A computer controls the heating.
   The heating _____ .

5 Uruguay won the first World Cup.
   The first World Cup _____

6 Van Gogh didn't paint this!
   This _____ !

7 Did Edison invent the telephone?
   Was _____?

Study Link **Student's Book p.138** *Grammar Bank 7D*

2 VOCABULARY verbs

Complete the sentences with the past participle of
these verbs.

name   create   write   ~~design~~   record
use   invent   make   base   discover

1 The Millennium Bridge in London was __designed__ by
   the architect Sir Norman Foster.

2 I was _____ after my grandmother.

3 Gold was _____ in California in 1848.

4 Copper and tin are _____ to make bronze.

5 Many different characters were _____ by
   Shakespeare.

6 Telephones weren't _____ until the late 1800s.

7 Most cakes are _____ from flour, eggs, sugar,
   and butter.

8 Many of the Beatles' songs were _____ at Abbey
   Road Studios in London.

9 *The Lord of the Rings* was _____ by JRR Tolkein.

10 Many characters in books are _____ on real people.

3 PRONUNCIATION -ed

a Circle the past participle with a different *-ed* sound.

🐕 /d/	/ɪd/	🐕 /d/	/ɪd/	👕 /t/
named	checked	appeared	rained	discovered
changed	separated	based	started	produced
(painted)	pretended	played	directed	missed

b Practise saying the words.

More Words to Learn

Write translations and try to remember the words.

Word	Pronunciation	Translation
bikini *noun*	/bɪˈkiːni/	
Biro *noun*	/ˈbaɪrəʊ/	
bullet-proof vest *noun*	/ˈbʊlɪtpruːf vest/	
dishwasher *noun*	/ˈdɪʃwɒʃə/	
light bulb *noun*	/laɪt bʌlb/	
nappies *noun*	/ˈnæpiz/	
stockings *noun*	/ˈstɒkɪŋz/	
Tipp-Ex *noun*	/ˈtɪpeks/	
vacuum cleaner *noun*	/ˈvækjuəm kliːnə/	
windscreen wipers *noun*	/ˈwɪndskriːn ˈwaɪpəz/	

Study idea

Sometimes you can remember new words by
visualizing them in your mind. Look at the words in
More Words to Learn and try to visualize the objects.

QUESTION TIME ?

Can you answer these questions?

1 Where were you born?
2 When was your house or flat built?
3 Who was your favourite film directed by?
4 How many languages are spoken in your country?
5 Which company was your mobile made by?

Study Link MultiROM

CAN YOU REMEMBER...? FILES 6&7

Complete each space with one word.

1 I'll do it tomorrow if I _____ time.
2 If I _____ you, I wouldn't buy that house.
3 I might _____ go out tonight. I'm very tired.
4 You _____ drink coffee at night – you won't sleep.
5 How _____ have you lived in this town?
6 How many films _____ Alfred Hitchcock make?
7 I _____ to smoke but I gave up last year.
8 Disposable nappies _____ invented by a woman.

1 BUYING TICKETS

Order the dialogue, 1–10.

A Return, please. How much is that? ☐

A Thanks. Oh, can I get anything to eat on the train? ☐

A Can I have a ticket to Glasgow, please? ☑ 1

A Good. And what time does it arrive? ☐

A Here you are. When does the next train leave? ☐

B That's £15.80. ☐

B It gets there at 12.15. ☐

B Yes, there's a trolley service with snacks and drinks. ☑ 10

B In ten minutes. ☐

B Single or return? ☐

2 SOCIAL ENGLISH

Complete the dialogues.

1 A I'm really l _ooking_ forward to our holiday.

   B Me too!

2 A Could you t_____ a photo of us, please?

   B Yes, of course. Are you r_____? Say cheese!

3 A You like chocolate, don't you?

   B Yes. W_____ do you ask?

   A Oh, no reason. I just w_____.

3 READING

a Read the information and circle the correct answer.

1 You **can** / (**can't**) buy a $10 ticket by credit card.

2 You **can** / **can't** use notes (bills) in the ticket machine.

3 You can store luggage **under** / **in front of** your seat.

4 You **can** / **can't** take bicycles on BART trains.

5 Many stations close **before** / **after** midnight.

6 A nine-year-old child can buy a $48 ticket for **$12** / **$24**.

7 You **have to** / **don't have to** pay for a three-year-old child.

8 Senior citizens **must** / **don't have to** carry ID.

BART – Bay Area Rapid Transit

GENERAL INFORMATION

BART ticket machines will accept nickels (five cents), dimes (ten cents), quarters (25 cents), $1, $5, $10, and $20 bills. Some ticket machines will accept credit cards for a minimum of $20 transaction.

When bringing luggage on a BART train, please try to keep aisles clear by storing your luggage under your seat. Some trains have space by the doors for wheelchairs or bikes. You can store your luggage there, but please keep it within your control at all times.

SERVICE HOURS

In many cases, BART service extends past midnight. Individual station closing times are coordinated with the schedule for the last train, beginning at around midnight.

SPECIAL TICKET TYPES

BART Blue – for frequent travellers

$32 / $48 / $64 tickets

BART Red – 75% discount

75% discount for persons with disabilities and children 5 to 12 years old, $32 ticket costs only $8!

Note: children 4 and under are FREE!

BART Green* – 75% discount

75% discount for senior citizens 65 years and older, $32 ticket costs only $8!

*Please note: When using BART Green Discount Tickets, seniors are required to carry proof of age.

b <u>Underline</u> five words or phrases you don't know. Use your dictionary to look up their meaning and pronunciation.

8 A

I hate weekends!

There aren't enough days in the weekend.
Rod Schmidt, American writer

1 GRAMMAR *something, anything, nothing,* etc.

a Circle the correct word.

1 I phoned twice, but **anybody** / (**nobody**) answered.

2 Do you know **anything** / **anyone** about this meeting?

3 Listen! I think **somebody** / **anybody** is upstairs.

4 He couldn't find his keys **nowhere** / **anywhere**.

5 We didn't know **someone** / **anyone** at the party.

6 Daniel has **something** / **anything** to tell you.

7 I'm sorry, I can't do **anything** / **nothing** about that.

8 We need to find **somewhere** / **anywhere** to stay.

9 We don't have **anywhere** / **nowhere** to put it.

b Look at the picture. Mark the sentences T (True) or F (False).

1 Nobody is dancing. _F_

2 There isn't anybody behind the bar. ___

3 There's nothing to eat. ___

4 The girl in the middle doesn't have anything on her feet. ___

5 There isn't anywhere to sit. ___

6 Someone is smoking. ___

7 The man on the right is saying something to the woman. ___

Study Link **Student's Book p.140** *Grammar Bank 8A*

2 PRONUNCIATION /e/, /əʊ/, /ʌ/

a Write the words in the chart.

~~sofa~~ ~~Sunday~~ ~~seven~~ help go stressful
n**o**thing d**o**n't cl**o**se n**o** l**u**nch n**e**ver
h**o**me st**u**dy b**u**tton b**e**st s**o**mething
anything

⏚	☎	⬆
seven	*sofa*	*Sunday*

b Practise saying the words.

3 VOCABULARY adjectives ending *-ed* and *-ing*

Complete the sentences with an adjective ending *-ed* or *-ing*.

1 I'm t _ired_ – I've had lots of really late nights!

2 Going to a spa at weekends is so r_____.

3 This film is really b_____. Turn the TV off.

4 She's very d_____. She's just lost her job.

5 I'm reading a really i_____ book.

6 Congratulations! That's really e_____ news.

7 Working ten hours every day is very t_____.

8 We always feel very r_____ on holiday.

9 Mum, I'm b_____! I want to go out.

10 The news at the moment is all very d_____.

11 He's very i_____ in archaeology.

12 The dogs were very e_____ to see us when we came home.

4 READING

Favourite times

What are your favourite times? And what times don't you like? Readers share their views.

I don't like ...

X I don't like my job, it's really boring, so I hate
¹ _Sunday evening_ . The thought of going to work
the next day is awful.

X I can't stand ² _____ in Britain. It's dark,
wet, cold, and depressing.

X I don't like ³ _____ much, I'm afraid.
Everybody eats too much, watches too much television,
and spends too much time with their families, and
nobody ever gives you anything you really want.

X I think it's the worst time of the week. After a relaxing
weekend I hate getting up on ⁴ _____ ,
with five days of work ahead of me.

I like ...

✓ I'm a teacher, so I love ⁵ _____ .
Sometimes I don't go anywhere on holiday, I just stay at
home – it's so relaxing having two months when you
don't have to think about work.

✓ There's a park near where I work, and I usually go for a
walk there at ⁶ _____ . The fresh air
helps me to get through the day.

✓ I always enjoy ⁷ _____ . It's a new start,
you can decide to live your life differently. But I never
do, of course ...

a Complete the text with these times.

Christmas	Monday morning	New Year's Eve
the winter	~~Sunday evening~~	the summer holidays
lunchtime		

b Underline five words you don't know. Use your
dictionary to look up their meaning and
pronunciation.

More Words to Learn

Write translations and try to remember the words.

Word	Pronunciation	Translation
day off *noun*	/deɪ ɒf/	
kids *noun*	/kɪdz/	
lift *noun*	/lɪft/	
exhausted *adjective*	/ɪgˈzɔːstɪd/	
latest (film) *adjective*	/ˈleɪtɪst/	
admit *verb*	/ədˈmɪt/	
exist *verb*	/ɪgˈzɪst/	
so (tired) *adverb*	/səʊ/	
except	/ɪkˈsept/	
on my own	/ɒn maɪ əʊn/	

Study idea

Be careful. Sometimes words have several meanings.
Use your dictionary to find other meanings for *so*
and *lift*.

QUESTION TIME ?

Can you answer these questions?

1 Does anybody in your family live abroad?

2 Have you bought anything today?

3 Is there anywhere to go swimming near where you live?

4 Do you know anyone who speaks more than two
languages?

5 Have you been anywhere on holiday this year?

Study Link MultiROM

Study Link www.oup.com/elt/englishfile/pre-intermediate

Old age is always 15 years older than I am.
Bernard Baruch, American political adviser

1 VOCABULARY

Complete the sentences with these words.

verdict	calendar	close	social	free
skin	diet	~~producer~~	water	stressed

1 Tariq is a record __producer__.

2 We use a _____ to find out what day and date it is.

3 I'm not relaxed. I'm very _____.

4 I only have two or three _____ friends.

5 What is the doctor's _____ about Tariq?

6 Tariq doesn't have much _____ time.

7 My _____ is quite healthy. I eat a lot of fruit.

8 My _____ life is great! I go out a lot.

9 You should always drink lots of _____.

10 I tan very easily – my _____ is quite dark.

2 GRAMMAR quantifiers, *too, not enough*

a Match the sentences.

1 I can't drive a car yet. ☑ *d*

2 I can't sleep. ☐

3 I'm very full. ☐

4 Can we stay the night here? ☐

5 I can't find my homework. ☐

6 My bag is really heavy. ☐

7 I'll never learn to drive now. ☐

8 I'll never finish this exam on time. ☐

a There are too many questions.

b I've eaten too much.

c There's too much paper on my desk.

d I'm too young.

e I'm too old!

f I'm too tired to drive home.

g There's too much noise.

h I have too many books in it.

b Circle the correct word or phrase for each sentence.

1 I can't pay. I don't have (enough money) / money enough.

2 This flat is tiny! Do you think it's **enough big / big enough** for both of us?

3 We couldn't go sailing yesterday. There wasn't **enough wind / wind enough**.

4 This coffee isn't **enough hot / hot enough**.

5 I know **a few / a little** words in Arabic.

6 I speak **a few / a little** Russian.

7 May I ask you **a few / a little** questions?

8 Could I have **a few / a little** more coffee, please?

9 If you can wait, we'll be there in **a few / a little** minutes.

10 Can I have **a few / a little** time to think, please?

Study Link **Student's Book p.140** *Grammar Bank 8B*

3 PRONUNCIATION /ʌ/, /uː/, /aɪ/, /e/

a Write the words in the chart.

~~young~~	friend	~~fruit~~	food	sunscreen	stress
month	wine	diet	exercise	studio	many

↑	*young*		
uː	*fruit*		
👁			
e			

b Practise saying the words.

69

4 READING

a Read the newspaper article and mark the sentences T (True) or F (False).

1 British children are fatter than they used to be.   *T*

2 Children don't see a lot of food advertisements.   ___

3 Children get less exercise than in the past.   ___

4 Children are overweight because they eat too much food.   ___

5 Children are overweight because they aren't doing enough exercise.   ___

6 It's important for young children to have a healthy diet.   ___

7 Parents should eat meals with their children.   ___

8 Playing on computers isn't very good for children.   ___

b Look at the highlighted words. What do you think they mean? Check with your dictionary.

Children's health

More Words to Learn

Write translations and try to remember the words.

Word	Pronunciation	Translation
diet *noun*	/'daɪət/	
skin *noun*	/skɪn/	
sunscreen *noun*	/'sʌnskriːn/	
close (friends) *adjective*	/kləʊs/	
fresh *adjective*	/freʃ/	
irritable *adjective*	/'ɪrɪtəbl/	
tense *adjective*	/tens/	
give up (smoking) *verb*	/gɪv ʌp/	
go wrong *verb*	/gəʊ rɒŋ/	
play squash *verb*	/pleɪ skwɒʃ/	

QUESTION TIME

Can you answer these questions?

1 Do you eat enough fruit and vegetables?

2 Do you think you have too much work?

3 Do you drink too much coffee or cola?

4 How much chocolate do you eat?

5 How many biscuits do you eat?

Study Link MultiROM

It's official – British children are getting fatter. According to a survey published in the British Medical Journal in 2001, nearly 16 per cent of two-year-olds are overweight and more than 20 per cent of four-year-olds are overweight. And since 2001, the problem has got worse. The government's latest health survey found that today about 30 per cent of all children are overweight.

WHY?

Children watch too much television, and they see ten food advertisements for every hour of TV they watch. They do less exercise, play less sport, and spend more time watching videos or playing computer games than they did in the past. The problem isn't that children eat too much food, or the wrong kind of food – though of course it's better to eat healthy foods than too much fat. The real problem is that too many children don't get any physical exercise.

WHAT CAN WE DO?

So how can we help our children develop a healthy attitude to food and exercise? Well, parents should try to help children to eat healthily when they're still young – we need to give children good habits at an early age. This means, for example, giving children fruit, not sweets, and eating meals together as a family if possible. Cooking with children is also a good idea, to teach them the importance of good food. A lot of children don't like vegetables, but even a few vegetables every day can help to improve their diet.

And instead of driving our children everywhere, we should encourage them to walk or cycle. We should make exercise interesting and exciting for them. Playing football in the park is much better for children than playing on the computer.

1 VOCABULARY phrasal verbs

a Complete what the people are saying in each picture.

1 Oh no! I forgot *to pick up* our passports.

2 _____ the music _____ – it's too loud!

3 Please _____ all your clothes _____ now!

4 You can _____ me _____ on 0208 2123 456.

5 _____ me _____ my bag!

6 It's awful! _____ it _____ to the shop.

b Complete the sentences with these verbs.

fill in	give up	go back	look after	look for
look up	take off	throw away	~~turn on~~	wake up

1 Every morning I *turn on* my computer and check
   my e-mail.

2 Please don't _____ me _____ too early
   tomorrow. I'm tired!

3 I've been ill, but I think I'll _____ to work tomorrow.

4 Remember to _____ your hat when you go inside.

5 I've lost my glasses. Can you help me _____ them?

6 I'm going to _____ my neighbour's cat this weekend.

7 My parents are trying to _____ smoking.

8 Which word did we need to _____ in the dictionary?

9 Please _____ the form and return it to me later.

10 Ugh! _____ that rubbish – it really smells!

Study Link **Student's Book p.153** *Vocabulary Bank*

2 GRAMMAR word order of phrasal verbs

a Circle the correct phrases. If both are possible, circle them both.

1 Please (fill in this form) / (fill this form in).

2 Your father's asleep. Don't **wake him up** / **wake up him**!

3 We **got at 6.30 up** / **got up at 6.30.**

4 You won't remember it if you don't **write it down /
   write down it.**

5 Why don't you **put your clothes away /
   put away your clothes?**

6 I'll **call you back** / **call back you** a bit later.

b Rewrite the sentences with a pronoun. Change the word order if necessary.

1 Can you turn up **the TV**?
   Can you turn it up?

2 I looked after **her children** for an hour.

   _____.

3 I'll give **your book** back tomorrow.

   _____.

4 Shall I look up **his address**?

   _____?

5 Have you thrown away **yesterday's newspaper**?

   _____?

6 He gets on with **his sisters** very well.

   _____.

Study Link **Student's Book p.140** *Grammar Bank 8C*

3 PRONUNCIATION /g/ and /dʒ/

a Write the words in the chart.

~~regular~~   vegetables   great   energetic
immigration   allergic   generally   glass

g	regular			
dʒ				

b Practise saying the words.

4 READING

a Read the article. Complete the gaps with these phrasal verbs.

get into   ~~put up~~   sit down   get on
turn on   get up   stay up

b Underline five words you don't know. Use your dictionary to look up their meaning and pronunciation.

Allergic to camping?

Seven reasons not to spend your weekend in a tent ...

1 It always rains, and everything gets wet – you, your tent, your sleeping bag, your clothes, and your food.

2 You always think you've ¹ _put up_ your tent in the best possible place. After the first night you realize that it was the worst possible place – on sharp rocks!

3 Your tent is so small that you can't stand up and you can't ² _____. All you can do is lie in your sleeping bag.

More Words to Learn

Write translations and try to remember the words.

Word	Pronunciation	Translation
alarm clock noun	/əˈlɑːm klɒk/	
gene noun	/dʒiːn/	
research noun	/rɪˈsɜːtʃ/	
active adjective	/ˈæktɪv/	
allergic adjective	/əˈlɜːdʒɪk/	
energetic adjective	/enəˈdʒetɪk/	
ready adjective	/ˈredi/	
discover verb	/dɪˈskʌvə/	
because of	/bɪˈkɒz əv/	
instead of	/ɪnˈsted əv/	

QUESTION TIME ?

Can you answer these questions?

1 Are you good at waking up in the morning?
2 What's the first thing you turn on in the morning?
3 Where do you look up words that you don't know?
4 If you're planning a journey, where do you find out about flights and hotels?
5 When was the last time you took something back to a shop?

Study Link MultiROM

4 Even if you ³_____ really well with your partner, after a day in a tent you won't speak to each other for a week.

5 The people next to you have a much bigger tent, with a barbecue and a TV. They ⁴_____ late enjoying themselves while you're trying to get to sleep.

6 A sheep tries to ⁵_____ your tent with you, but fails. However, a hundred insects have already successfully got into your tent with you.

7 After a bad night's sleep, things are no better when you ⁶_____ in the morning. No coffee, no tea, no newspapers, and the people in the next tent ⁷_____ their TV again.

The only good thing is that it's very cheap. But of course it's cheap – nobody would pay much for this.

There are two things in life for which we are never truly prepared: Twins.

Josh Billings, American comedian

1 GRAMMAR *so, neither* + auxiliaries

a Complete the conversation with words from the box.

~~am~~ so would neither were

A Hi, Sue. What are you doing on Saturday?

B I'm going to that lecture on 'finding out about your family'.

A So ¹ _*am*_ I. I'm not sure how much we'll learn though.

B ² _____ am I. But I want to learn more about my great-grandparents.

A ³ _____ do I. Mine were born at the end of the 19th century!

B So ⁴ _____ mine. Did they live in London?

A Yes, they did. I'd love to find out more about other members of the family too.

B So ⁵ _____ I. Let's go together. I'll pick you up at eight.

A OK. See you then.

b Agree with the statements.

1 I love dancing.

So do I.

2 I hated our school uniform.

_____ .

3 I don't have any money.

_____ .

4 I'm not sure what the answer is.

_____ .

5 I can play the guitar.

_____ .

6 I've only been there once.

_____ .

7 I would love to go to Australia.

_____ .

8 I went camping last year.

_____ .

Study Link **Student's Book p.140** *Grammar Bank 8D*

2 VOCABULARY similarities

Complete the text with words from the box.

as both (x2) like neither so (x2) ~~similar~~

In our family, we all look quite ¹ _*similar*_ . I have dark hair and dark eyes and ² _____ do my parents and brother and sister. My brother and sister ³ _____ have big noses, and my mouth is exactly the same ⁴ _____ my sister's.

I think I look ⁵ _____ my mum – we are ⁶ _____ quite tall. We also like and dislike the same things. I love old books and ⁷ _____ does she, and I don't like sport and ⁸ _____ does she. People often think we're sisters, not mother and daughter!

3 PRONUNCIATION word stress

a Underline the stressed syllable in these words.

1 id<u>en</u>tical 6 political

2 adopt 7 investigate

3 baby 8 personality

4 student 9 medical

5 exercise 10 romantic

b Practise saying the words.

4 READING

a Read the interview and mark the sentences
T (True), F (False), or ? (Doesn't say).

1 Michelle is 18 years old.   *F*

2 Catherine and Michelle are always together.   ___

3 They have the same hobbies.   ___

4 Catherine always knows how Michelle is feeling. ___

5 They like the same films.   ___

6 They live in the same city.   ___

7 They're good at all the same things.   ___

8 Catherine doesn't like having a twin sister.   ___

Catherine Orr is 19 and is a non-identical twin. She tells us about her relationship with her sister, Michelle.

Don't call us 'the twins'!

How do you think it is different being a twin?

I think it's very different. We've been through exactly the same things: the same birthdays, the same parties, the same first day at school, the same evil maths teacher.

Do you think you and Michelle are more similar than ordinary sisters?

Definitely. If I don't like a film, then neither does she. We pick up the phone at the same time to call each other. If I get ill, so does she.

Do you get on well with Michelle now?

Yes, I see her about once a week, although it doesn't make much difference if we see each other or not. We always know how the other is feeling. I think it's hard not to be close when you have known someone your whole life.

What were the best things about being a twin as a child? And now?

You have someone who knows you almost as well as you know yourself, someone who is experiencing all the same things as you. Now it's great because we have almost exactly the same memories. She is my memory sometimes.

What were the worst things?

People called us 'the twins' as if we were one person – I hated that, and so did Michelle. Some people also used to save money and buy one birthday present for both of us! Also Michelle was good at sport and I was terrible – that was difficult for me.

b Underline five words you don't know. Use your dictionary to check their meaning and pronunciation.

More Words to Learn

Write translations and try to remember the words.

Word	Pronunciation	Translation
beliefs *noun*	/bɪˈliːfs/	
twins *noun*	/twɪnz/	
wood *noun*	/wʊd/	
(be) adopted *adjective*	/əˈdɒptɪd/	
amazing *adjective*	/əˈmeɪzɪŋ/	
convinced *adjective*	/kənˈvɪnst/	
enormous *adjective*	/ɪˈnɔːməs/	
identical *adjective*	/aɪˈdentɪkl/	
vote (for) *verb*	/vəʊt/	
reunited	/riːjuːˈnaɪtɪd/	

QUESTION TIME

Are you the same or different? Can you respond to these people?

1 'I like going on holiday.'

2 'I don't speak Chinese.'

3 'I love the weekend.'

4 'I don't know what to do tonight.'

5 'I want to speak English well.'

Study Link MultiROM

CAN YOU REMEMBER...?   FILES 7&8

Complete each space with one word.

1 I've worked for this company _____ ten years.

2 How many films _____ Quentin Tarantino made?

3 I didn't _____ to like jazz, but now I love it.

4 The *Sherlock Holmes* books were _____ by Arthur Conan Doyle.

5 We didn't do _____ at the weekend. We stayed at home.

6 The doctor said that I drink too _____ coffee.

7 It's very cold today. Put your coat _____.

8 A I love Paris.   B _____ do I!

Study Link www.oup.com/elt/englishfile/pre-intermediate

1 MAKING PHONE CALLS

Match the beginnings and endings.

1 Who's   *d*
2 I'm sorry. I've
3 Can I speak
4 Just a moment, I'll
5 I'm sorry. The
6 Don't worry,
7 Hello? Is
8 Could I leave
9 I'll call

a   put you through.
b   line's busy.
c   that Claudia?
d   calling?
e   a message for her?
f   I'll hold.
g   back in ten minutes.
h   got the wrong number.
i   to Claudia, please?

2 SOCIAL ENGLISH

Circle the correct words.

1 Thanks for all / (everything). I've had a wonderful time.
2 Look at the sunset. Isn't that / there amazing?
3 A Oh no!
   B What's / How's the matter?
4 Cheers / Health! To us!
5 A We're going to work together!
   B I'm not / I don't believe it.

3 READING

a Read the text. Which sentence is the best summary?

1 British and American English are almost exactly the same.
2 The most important difference between British and American English is the vocabulary.
3 Travellers don't have problems understanding British and American English.

American and British English

If you've learnt British English and you're travelling in the States, or if you've learnt American English and you're travelling in Britain, you'll notice some differences. An obvious difference is the accent, but most travellers find that they don't have too many problems with this. There are some grammatical differences, but they shouldn't make it difficult to understand people, or to communicate. That leaves differences in vocabulary, which can cause misunderstandings. Sometimes the difference is only the spelling, for example, in British English *centre*, *colour*, and *travelled*, and in American English *center*, *color*, and *traveled*. But sometimes the word is completely different in British and American English, and it's a good idea to be prepared.

Can you match the British and American words?

1 bill   *k*   a fries
2 chips   b freeway
3 ground floor   c vacation
4 holiday   d mail
5 lift   e round trip ticket
6 motorway   f zip code
7 nappies   g diapers
8 petrol   h first floor
9 post   i stand in line
10 postcode   j one-way ticket
11 queue (v)   k check
12 return ticket   l cab
13 single ticket   m elevator
14 taxi   n gas

b Underline five words or phrases you don't know. Make sure you can say them in British and American English.

9 A What a week!

*My advisers built a wall between myself and my people. I didn't realize
what was happening. When I woke up, I had lost my people.*
Mohammed Reza Pahlavi, ex Shah of Iran

1 GRAMMAR past perfect

a Complete the sentences with the past perfect form of the verbs in brackets.

1 My plants were dead because my neighbour
   hadn't watered them. (not water)

2 I couldn't get into my flat because I
   _____ my key. (forget)

3 The teacher was angry because we
   _____ our homework. (not do)

4 The man lent me his newspaper after he
   _____ it. (read)

5 They got to the cinema after the film
   _____. (start)

b Write questions in the past perfect.

1 **A** I saw *Titanic* at the weekend.
   B you / see it / before
   Had you seen it before?

2 **A** I finished *The Lord of the Rings* last week.
   B you / read it / before
   _____?

3 **A** My parents were in Paris last weekend.
   B they / be there / before
   _____?

4 **A** We ate some snails last night.
   B you / eat them / before
   _____?

5 **A** Charles flew a plane last week.
   B he / fly one / before
   _____?

c Make these two sentences into one. Use the past perfect and the past simple.

1 I turned off the light. After that I got into bed.
   After ___*I had turned off the light, I got into bed*___.

2 Cindy got dressed. Then she went to work.
   After Cindy _____.

3 I saw the film. Then I read the book.
   After _____.

4 Ben copied my notes. After that he gave them back to me.
   When Ben _____.

5 Kathy and Tom did some exercise. Then they had a shower.
   After Kathy and Tom _____.

d Circle the correct verb.

When I introduced Sue and Tim at my party, they were sure they [1] met / (had met) before. They [2] **finally discovered** / **had finally discovered** they [3] **were** / **had been** on the same holiday the year before.

I was looking for my mobile yesterday morning, but I couldn't find it. I was sure I [4] **didn't lose** / **hadn't lost** it, because I [5] **saw** / **had seen** it twenty minutes before. Then I realized that I [6] **left** / **had left** it in my trouser pocket, and I [7] **put** / **had put** my trousers in the washing machine!

76

Last week my neighbour was on holiday. One night I ⁸ **heard / had heard** a strange noise in her house. I ⁹ **went / had gone** to have a look, and I found that someone ¹⁰ **broke / had broken** into the house. Luckily, he (or she!) ¹¹ **already left / had already left** when I got there, and they ¹² **didn't steal / hadn't stolen** much – just the TV.

Study Link **Student's Book p.142** *Grammar Bank 9A*

2 PRONUNCIATION vowel sounds

a Write the words in the correct group.

week	name	behave	hit	fast	people
asked	sit	hospital	gave	last	screamed

week			

b Practise saying the words.

3 VOCABULARY adverbs

Complete the stories with these words.

luckily	unfortunately	accidentally	suddenly (x2)
immediately (x2)	~~strangely~~		

The other day I realized that people were looking at me very ¹ *strangely* . I couldn't think why. Then I ² _____ realized that I'd ³ _____ gone out with my slippers on! I ⁴ _____ went home and put my shoes on instead.

We nearly had an accident last month. The car in front of us ⁵ _____ stopped for no reason. ⁶ _____ we stopped before we hit it, but ⁷ _____ my sister hit the windscreen and cut her head. We took her to hospital ⁸ _____ .

More Words to Learn

Write translations and try to remember the words.

Word	Pronunciation	Translation
fine *noun*	/faɪn/	
motorway *noun*	/ˈməʊtəweɪ/	
porter *noun*	/ˈpɔːtə/	
arrest *verb*	/əˈrest/	
behave *verb*	/bɪˈheɪv/	
commit a crime *verb*	/kəˈmɪt ə kraɪm/	
jump *verb*	/dʒʌmp/	
rob *verb*	/rɒb/	
scream *verb*	/skriːm/	
snore *verb*	/snɔː/	

QUESTION TIME ?

Can you complete these sentences with the past perfect?

1 I passed the exam easily because …
2 I didn't want to see the film because …
3 The teacher was angry with me because …
4 I couldn't take any photos because …
5 I wasn't very hungry because …

Study Link **MultiROM**

Study Link www.oup.com/elt/englishfile/pre-intermediate **77**

Women still remember the first kiss after men have forgotten the last.

Remy de Gourmont, French writer

Then he kissed me

1 GRAMMAR reported speech

a Complete the reported speech.

Direct speech	Reported speech
1 ' I live in a small flat. '	She said she *lived in a small flat* .
2 ' I don't like it much. '	He told me he _____ .
3 ' I'm studying English. '	She told me she _____ .
4 ' I've been to New York. '	He told me he _____ .
5 ' I haven't read the paper. '	She said she _____ .
6 ' I woke up really early. '	He said he _____ .
7 ' I got home at 11.00. '	She told me she _____ .
8 ' I won't forget. '	He said he _____ .

b Change the questions from direct speech to reported speech.

1 'Would you like a coffee?'

He asked me if I wanted a coffee.

2 'Are you a new student?'

He asked me _____ .

3 'Have you been here long?'

He asked me _____ .

4 'Where do your parents live?'

_____ .

5 'What are you studying?'

_____ .

6 'Where did you go to school?'

_____ .

7 'Are you interested in computers?'

_____ .

8 'What's your mobile number?'

_____ .

c Write what the people said.

1 He asked me if I wanted a drink.

'__Do__ you __want__ a drink?'

2 They said that they didn't like their boss.

'We _____ _____ our boss.'

3 I said that I would talk to him later.

'I _____ _____ to you later.'

4 We told him that we could take him to the station.

'We _____ _____ you to the station.'

5 She said that she had broken the glass.

'I _____ _____ the glass.'

6 I asked him what he would do next.

'What _____ you _____ next?'

7 He told me that he didn't want to come to the party.

'I _____ _____ to come to the party.'

8 You said that you'd wait for me.

'I _____ _____ for you.'

Study Link **Student's Book p.142** *Grammar Bank 9B*

2 VOCABULARY say, tell, or ask?

a Circle the correct words.

1 I **said** / **told** the shop assistant I was very unhappy with my new TV.

2 'Where's the swimming pool?' she **told** / **asked**.

3 She **said** / **told** that she would meet me at 7.00 p.m.

4 He **told** / **asked** me if I would go out with him.

5 'I'm really sorry,' **said** / **told** Jill.

6 The taxi driver **asked** / **told** me if I wanted a receipt.

b Complete the sentences with *said*, *told*, or *asked*.

1 We _____told_____ our teacher that we would be late for class.

2 You _____ you'd be there at lunchtime.

3 I _____ you that the computer didn't work.

4 We _____ him if he wanted to go to the cinema with us.

5 He _____ me he would be late.

6 I _____ the receptionist if there were any messages for me.

3 PRONUNCIATION rhyming verbs

a Circle the verbs that rhyme in each group.

1 (read)   (went)   heard

2 saw   made   caught

3 lost   stood   should

4 paid   said   made

5 meant   preferred   heard

6 cried   tried   lived

7 told   tore   sold

b Practise saying the verbs.

More Words to Learn

Write translations and try to remember the words.

Word	Pronunciation	Translation
bride *noun*	/braɪd/	
hold *verb*	/həʊld/	
let (somebody) know *verb*	/let nəʊ/	
shine *verb*	/faɪn/	
<u>wh</u>isper *verb*	/ˈwɪspə/	
<u>a</u>lmost *adverb*	/ˈɔːlməʊst/	
tight *adverb*	/taɪt/	
by your side	/baɪ jɔː saɪd/	

1 GRAMMAR

a 1 not to have   2 to meet
  3 not to worry   4 to close   5 not to tell
  6 to relax   7 to take

b 1 important to be
  2 careful not to drop
  3 dangerous to swim
  4 difficult to sleep
  5 interesting to talk to
  6 nice to see
  7 easy to use

c 1 to study   2 to learn   3 to buy
  4 to have   5 to make   6 to take
  7 to argue   8 to meet

2 VOCABULARY

I'm Bill. I'm 16 and I've decided **to** leave school. I'm going **to** leave next week. I'm hoping **to** get a job with computers because I'm planning **to** make lots of money.

I've tried **to** work hard but I'm not a very good student. All the other students understand and learn **to** do things quickly but not me. And I never remember **to** bring my books to class and always forget **to** do my homework.

I'd like **to** learn **to** fly because I want **to** be a pilot. But first I need **to** do a course. My mother offered **to** pay for the course but only if I promised **to** finish school!

3 PRONUNCIATION

a 1 r<u>e</u>member   2 r<u>e</u>ception   3 sur<u>vive</u>
  4 de<u>ci</u>de   5 pre<u>ten</u>d   6 t<u>o</u>m<u>o</u>rrow
  7 ad<u>vice</u>   8 es<u>ca</u>pe

4 READING

a 1 F   2 F   3 T   4 F   5 T   6 T

1 GRAMMAR

a 1 tidying   2 going   3 making
  4 eating   5 talking   6 travelling

b 1 c   2 a   3 e   4 f   5 d   6 b

c 1 Writing   2 sending   3 imagining
  4 driving   5 listening   6 Staying
  7 reading   8 getting up   9 taking
  10 going   11 getting   12 having
  13 Turning   14 leaving

d 1 to get   2 to stop   3 working
  4 to set up   5 cooking   6 to open
  7 to spend   8 learning   9 getting up
  10 catching   11 travelling   12 working
  13 sailing   14 surfing   15 to move
  16 teaching   17 to be

2 PRONUNCIATION

a 1 <u>sing</u>ing   2 <u>lang</u>uage   3 <u>morn</u>ing
  4 <u>listen</u>ing   5 en<u>joy</u>ing   6 re<u>lax</u>ing
  7 re<u>mem</u>bering   8 pre<u>ten</u>ding

3 VOCABULARY

1 c   2 d   3 f   4 a   5 e   6 b

1 GRAMMAR

a 1 have to   2 don't have to
  3 doesn't have to   4 has to   5 have to
  6 don't have to   7 Does, have to, have to
  8 Does, have to, have to

b 1 You must fasten your safety belt.
  2 You must stop here.
  3 You mustn't smoke.
  4 You must turn left.
  5 You must wear a helmet.
  6 You mustn't walk on the grass.

c 1 don't have to   2 mustn't
  3 don't have to   4 mustn't   5 mustn't
  6 don't have to

2 PRONUNCIATION

a 1 mus/t/n't   2 lis/t/en   3 ha/l/f
  4 We/d/nesday   5 /k/nees   6 /k/now
  7 w/h/ile   8 si/g/n   8 wa/l/k

3 VOCABULARY

1 British and American English are very similar.
2 English pronunciation can be quite difficult.
3 Learning Japanese isn't very easy.
4 I think Hungarian is incredibly complicated.
5 Czech is a bit easier.
6 Reading is a really useful way to learn vocabulary.

4 READING

b 1 Ana   2 Péter, Sompong   3 Konrad
  4 Elke   5 Péter

1 VOCABULARY

a 1 football   2 baseball   3 swimming
  4 skiing   5 volleyball   6 tennis
  7 rugby   8 aerobics   9 cycling
  10 golf

b 1 play   2 go   3 plays   4 go
  5 does   6 play

c 1 skiing   2 baseball   3 basketball
  4 volleyball   5 swimming

d 1 down   2 round   3 through
  4 over   5 through

2 GRAMMAR

a 1 is running across   2 is going through
  3 is cycling up   4 are skiing down
  5 is getting out of   6 are rowing round

b 1 round   2 out of   3 to   4 into
  5 along   6 under   7 past   8 through
  9 along   10 towards   11 across

3 PRONUNCIATION

/ɒ/ over
/ə/ through
/aʊ/ under

CAN YOU REMEMBER…?

1 been   2 hasn't   3 more   4 most   5 to
6 doing   7 mustn't   8 out

PRACTICAL ENGLISH 5

1 TAKING SOMETHING BACK

1 bought   2 decided   3 tried   4 too
5 refund   6 here

2 SOCIAL ENGLISH

1 What, think   2 Never   3 lovely
4 would, like   5 good, idea   6 lost

3 READING

a 1 latest   2 boutiques   3 overlooks
  4 won't break the bank   5 crowds
  6 huge

b 1 Borders   2 Borders
  3 Banana Republic   4 Virgin Megastore
  5 Camper   6 Borders

6 A — WORKBOOK KEY

1 GRAMMAR

a 1 c   2 a   3 f   4 b   5 e   6 d

b 1 take   2 will break   3 hear   4 stay
5 will be   6 see   7 'll get   8 will feel

c 1 D   2 C   3 F   4 A   5 G   6 B   7 E

d 1 puts, will come
2 see, will have
3 walk, will have
4 throw, make, will come
5 dig, will find
6 break, will have
7 flies, will have, kill, will have, will be

2 VOCABULARY

1 wearing, carrying   2 won, earned
3 say, told   4 hoping, waited
5 watched, look at   6 known, met
7 make, do   8 look, look, look like

3 PRONUNCIATION

a 1 b   2 e   3 f   4 c   5 a   6 d

6 B — WORKBOOK KEY

1 GRAMMAR

a 1 had, would drive
2 saw, would be
3 wouldn't know, found
4 would, do, lost
5 were, would come
6 would buy, had

b 1 If I saw a shark, I'd be very
frightened.
2 What would you do if you saw a fire?
3 He'd go sailing if he could swim.
4 If she won the lottery, she'd buy lots
of new clothes.
5 What would people do if they
couldn't watch TV?
6 I'd go to the doctor's if I were you.

2 PRONUNCIATION

a 1 open, chicken, insect
2 about, afraid, attack
3 finally, animal, crocodile
4 direction, mosquito, safari

3 VOCABULARY

Across: 1 bear   3 tiger   4 elephant
7 sheep

Down: 1 butterfly   2 lion   3 eagle
6 horse

4 READING

b Sentence 2

6 C — WORKBOOK KEY

1 GRAMMAR

a 1 might go   2 might get
3 might continue   4 might rent
5 might live   6 might share
7 might not want   8 might fail
9 might have to

b 1 might   2 may not   3 might
4 might   5 may not   6 might   7 might
8 may not

2 PRONUNCIATION

a 1 organization   2 invitation   3 election
4 information   5 imagination
6 translation   7 communication
8 decision

3 VOCABULARY

a **Verb:** communicate, conclude, correct,
confuse, demonstrate, inject, organize,
predict

Noun: communication, conclusion,
correction, confusion, demonstration,
injection, organization, prediction

b 1 conclusion   2 communicate
3 injection   4 demonstration
5 prediction   6 organize

4 READING

a 1 T   2 F   3 T   4 F   5 T   6 T
7 F   8 T

6 D — WORKBOOK KEY

1 GRAMMAR

a 1 should, B
2 should, F
3 shouldn't, A
4 shouldn't, E
5 shouldn't, D
6 should, C

b 1 should tell   2 shouldn't be
3 shouldn't go   4 should go
5 should buy   6 should join
7 shouldn't watch

c 1 D   2 F   3 A   4 B   5 C   6 G   7 E

2 PRONUNCIATION

a 1 would   2 should   3 could
4 understood   5 good

3 VOCABULARY

1 getting, worse   2 got, e-mails
3 get, angry   4 get, tickets   5 get, on
6 gets, home   7 get, married
8 is getting, taller   9 'm getting, off
10 got, lost

CAN YOU REMEMBER...?

1 to   2 having   3 don't   4 through
5 won't   6 would   7 might / may
8 should

PRACTICAL ENGLISH 6

1 ASKING FOR MEDICINE

1 help   2 hurts   3 have   4 Are   5 think
6 might   7 take   8 times   9 often
10 much

2 SOCIAL ENGLISH

1 Bless
2 How, sounds, shall, mind, choose
3 sorry, pity

3 READING

a 1 You must keep this medicine
somewhere safe.
2 You should be careful not to take too
much of this medicine.
3 You have to turn your mobile off.
4 You should be careful with your
belongings.
5 You mustn't smoke here.
6 You should be careful or you might
fall over.
7 You shouldn't leave anything valuable
in your car.
8 You shouldn't drink this water.
9 You must make sure that the door is
never left open.
10 You should be very careful if you're
driving here.
11 You have to wait until a waiter shows
you where to sit.
12 You mustn't use radios in this park.

7 A — WORKBOOK KEY

1 VOCABULARY

1 frightened   2 terrified   3 wasps, spiders
4 panic   5 closed spaces   6 heights

2 GRAMMAR

a 1 since   2 for   3 for   4 since
5 Since, for   6 since   7 since
8 For, since

b 1 since   2 for   3 since   4 for   5 for
6 since   7 for   8 for   9 since   10 since

c 1 How long have, lived
2 When did, move out
3 How long have, been
4 How long has, been
5 When did, become
6 How long has, been
7 When did, get

d 1 Gill *has lived* here for seven years.
2 How long *has she been* a professional dancer?
3 They *have been married* since 2000.
4 He has been in France *since* February.
5 How long *have you had* your car?
6 He's had this job *for* eight years.
7 She *has had* three homes since she was born.
8 My parents *lived / have lived* in the same house for many years.

3 PRONUNCIATION

a 1 /ɪ/ 2 /ɪ/ 3 /aɪ/ 4 /aɪ/ 5 /aɪ/ 6 /ɪ/
7 /aɪ/ 8 /ɪ/

7 B WORKBOOK KEY

1 VOCABULARY

1 c 2 d 3 g 4 e 5 b 6 h 7 f 8 a

2 PRONUNCIATION

a **Stress on 2nd syllable:** su<u>cc</u>essful, ca<u>reer</u>, ap<u>pear</u>, di<u>rect</u>, di<u>rec</u>tor

Stress on 1st syllable: <u>fa</u>mous, <u>ci</u>nema, <u>vi</u>olence, <u>ti</u>cket, <u>ac</u>tor

3 GRAMMAR

a 1 've known 2 were 3 met 4 were
5 've been 6 went 7 were 8 chose
9 told 10 've been 11 've shared

b 1 have, lived 2 got, were
3 left, 've worked 4 did, go, took
5 have, had, bought
6 haven't seen, moved

4 READING

a 1, 6, 3, 7, 5, 4, 2

b 1 was 2 did his family move
3 did he see 4 did he work
5 has he been married

c 1 In 1941. / On January 5, 1941.
2 In 1952.
3 (When he was) at secondary school.
4 For eight years (from 1963 to 1971).
5 For 40 years. / Since 1965.

7 C WORKBOOK KEY

1 GRAMMAR

a 1 Did you use to enjoy
2 didn't use to like
3 used to be
4 Did Colin use to work
5 didn't use to be
6 used to live
7 didn't use to do
8 Did he use to play

b 1 used 2 used to 3 didn't use to
4 Did you use to 5 used
6 Did your children use to

2 PRONUNCIATION

a /z/ used to
/s/ friends
/tʃ/ school
/dʒ/ great

3 VOCABULARY

1 c 2 g 3 e 4 b 5 a 6 f 7 h 8 d

4 READING

a 1 Where did you go to school?
2 Did you ever get into trouble?
3 What subjects were you good at?
4 Did you have a favourite teacher?
5 What did you want to do when you were young?
6 What's the most important lesson you've learned in life?

b 1 T 2 ? 3 F 4 ? 5 T 6 F
7 F 8 T

7 D WORKBOOK KEY

1 GRAMMAR

a 1 Aspirin is used to relieve pain.
2 The sandwich was named after the Earl of Sandwich.
3 St Paul's Cathedral was designed by Christopher Wren.
4 This film is based on a true story.
5 The first crossword puzzle was published in 1913.
6 The first credit card was issued by the Diner's Club.
7 The fax machine is not used very often these days.
8 Penicillin was discovered by Alexander Fleming.

b 1 President Kennedy was assassinated in 1963.
2 Champagne is made in France.
3 What is your dog called?
4 Television was invented by John Logie Baird.
5 This room is cleaned every morning.
6 Her flat was designed by a famous architect.
7 Stamps are only sold in the Post Office.
8 Where were those shoes made?

c 1 I was stopped by the police last night.
2 *Crocodile Rock* was sung by Elton John.
3 All the photographs at our wedding were taken by my cousin.
4 The heating is controlled by a computer.
5 The first World Cup was won by Uruguay.
6 This wasn't painted by Van Gogh!
7 Was the telephone invented by Edison?

2 VOCABULARY

1 designed 2 named 3 discovered
4 used 5 created 6 invented 7 made
8 recorded 9 written 10 based

3 PRONUNCIATION

a /d/ painted, based
/ɪd/ checked, rained
/t/ discovered

CAN YOU REMEMBER...?

1 have 2 were 3 not 4 shouldn't
5 long 6 did 7 used 8 were

PRACTICAL ENGLISH 7

1 BUYING TICKETS

Return, please. How much is that? 3
Thanks. Oh, can I get anything to eat on the train? 9
Can I have a ticket to Glasgow, please? 1
Good. And what time does it arrive? 7
Here you are. When does the next train leave? 5
That's £15.80. 4
It gets there at 12.15. 8
Yes, there's a trolley service with snacks and drinks. 10
In ten minutes. 6
Single or return? 2

2 SOCIAL ENGLISH

1 looking 2 take, ready
3 Why, wondered

3 READING

a 1 can't 2 can 3 under 4 can
5 after 6 $12 7 don't have to
8 must

8 A — WORKBOOK KEY

1 GRAMMAR

a 1 nobody 2 anything 3 somebody
4 anywhere 5 anyone 6 something
7 anything 8 somewhere 9 anywhere

b 1 F 2 T 3 F 4 T 5 F 6 T 7 T

2 PRONUNCIATION

a /e/ seven, help, stressful, never, best,
anything

/əʊ/ sofa, go, don't, close, no, home

/ʌ/ Sunday, nothing, lunch, study,
button, something

3 VOCABULARY

1 tired 2 relaxing 3 boring
4 depressed 5 interesting 6 exciting
7 tiring 8 relaxed 9 bored
10 depressing 11 interested 12 excited

4 READING

a 1 Sunday evening 2 the winter
3 Christmas 4 Monday morning
5 the summer holidays 6 lunchtime
7 New Year's Eve

8 B — WORKBOOK KEY

1 VOCABULARY

1 producer 2 calendar 3 stressed
4 close 5 verdict 6 free 7 diet
8 social 9 water 10 skin

2 GRAMMAR

a 1 d 2 g 3 b 4 f 5 c 6 h 7 e 8 a

b 1 enough money 2 big enough
3 enough wind 4 hot enough 5 a few
6 a little 7 a few 8 a little 9 a few
10 a little

3 PRONUNCIATION

a /ʌ/ young, sunscreen, month
/uː/ fruit, food, studio
/aɪ/ wine, diet, exercise
/e/ friend, stress, many

4 READING

a 1 T 2 F 3 T 4 F 5 T 6 T
7 T 8 T

8 C — WORKBOOK KEY

1 VOCABULARY

a 1 to pick up 2 Turn, down 3 pick, up
4 call, back 5 Give, back 6 Take, back

b 1 turn on 2 wake, up 3 go back
4 take off 5 look for 6 look after
7 give up 8 look up 9 fill in
10 throw away

2 GRAMMAR

a 1 fill in this form / fill this form in
2 wake him up
3 got up at 6.30
4 write it down
5 put your clothes away / put away
your clothes
6 call you back

b 1 Can you turn it up?
2 I looked after them for an hour.
3 I'll give it back (to you) tomorrow.
4 Shall I look it up?
5 Have you thrown it away?
6 He gets on with them very well. /
He gets on very well with them.

3 PRONUNCIATION

a /g/ regular, great, immigration, glass
/dʒ/ vegetables, energetic, allergic,
generally

4 READING

a 1 put up 2 sit down 3 get on
4 stay up 5 get into 6 get up
7 turn on

8 D — WORKBOOK KEY

1 GRAMMAR

a 1 am 2 Neither 3 So 4 were
5 would

b 1 So do I.
2 So did I.
3 Neither do I.
4 Neither am I.
5 So can I.
6 So have I.
7 So would I.
8 So did I.

2 VOCABULARY

1 similar 2 so 3 both 4 as 5 like
6 both 7 so 8 neither

3 PRONUNCIATION

a 1 identical 2 adopt 3 baby
4 student 5 exercise 6 political
7 investigate 8 personality 9 medical
10 romantic

4 READING

a 1 F 2 F 3 ? 4 T 5 T 6 ?
7 F 8 F

CAN YOU REMEMBER...?

1 for 2 has 3 use 4 written
5 anything 6 much 7 on 8 So

PRACTICAL ENGLISH 8

1 MAKING PHONE CALLS

1 d 2 h 3 i 4 a 5 b 6 f 7 c
8 e 9 g

2 SOCIAL ENGLISH

1 everything 2 that 3 What's
4 Cheers 5 I don't

3 READING

a Sentence 2

1 k 2 a 3 h 4 c 5 m 6 b 7 g
8 n 9 d 10 f 11 i 12 e 13 j 14 l

9 A — WORKBOOK KEY

1 GRAMMAR

a 1 hadn't watered 2 'd forgotten
3 hadn't done 4 'd read 5 had started

b 1 Had you seen it before?
2 Had you read it before?
3 Had they been there before?
4 Had you eaten them before?
5 Had he flown one before?

c 1 After I had turned off the light, I got
into bed.
2 After Cindy had got dressed, she
went to work.
3 After I had seen the film, I read the
book.
4 When Ben had copied my notes, he
gave them back to me.
5 After Kathy and Tom had done some
exercise, they had a shower.

d 1 had met 2 finally discovered
3 had been 4 hadn't lost 5 had seen
6 had left 7 had put 8 heard 9 went
10 had broken 11 had already left
12 hadn't stolen

2 PRONUNCIATION

a /iː/ week, people, screamed
/ɑː/ fast, asked, last
/eɪ/ name, behave, gave
/ɪ/ hit, sit, hospital

3 VOCABULARY

1 strangely 2 suddenly 3 accidentally
4 immediately 5 suddenly 6 Luckily
7 unfortunately 8 immediately

9 B WORKBOOK KEY

1 GRAMMAR

a 1 lived in a small flat
2 didn't like it much
3 was studying English
4 had been to New York
5 hadn't read the paper
6 had woken up really early
7 had got home at 11.00
8 wouldn't forget

b 1 He asked me if I wanted a coffee.
2 He asked me if I was a new student.
3 He asked me if I'd been there long.
4 He asked me where my parents lived.
5 He asked me what I was studying.
6 He asked me where I'd gone to school.
7 He asked me if I was interested in computers.
8 He asked me what my mobile number was.

c 1 Do, want 2 don't like 3 'll talk
4 can take 5 've broken 6 will, do
7 don't want 8 'll wait

2 VOCABULARY

a 1 told 2 asked 3 said 4 asked
5 said 6 asked

b 1 told 2 said 3 told 4 asked
5 told 6 asked

3 PRONUNCIATION

a 1 read, went
2 saw, caught
3 stood, should
4 paid, made
5 preferred, heard
6 cried, tried
7 told, sold

CAN YOU REMEMBER...?

1 nobody 2 many 3 them 4 did
5 had 6 gone 7 was 8 if

New English File Pre-intermediate online

 Grammar
Practise your grammar with exercises for each File.

 Vocabulary
Practise your vocabulary with exercises for each File.

 Pronunciation
Practise the sounds of English, and play sounds and word stress games.

 Audio Words
Listen to the words, learn them, and add your translation.

 Practical English
Listen to and learn phrases, and do 'spot the mistake' activities.

 Learning Record
Download the Study Link Learning Record (PDF, size 109 KB).

 Text Builder
Read and complete texts from the Student's Book.

 Weblinks
Links to websites for learning more about the topics in New English File Pre-intermediate.

 Games
Have some fun with our games – and learn English at the same time!

 Mini Phrasebook
Download two pages of Practical English for travelling. You can get this in colour (PDF, size 139 KB) or black and white (PDF, size 97 KB)

Vocabulary Calendar
Write down and learn new words every month.
Download this month's calendar (PDF, size 32 KB)

Don't forget that New English File has a website for you at: www.oup.com/elt/englishfile/pre-intermediate
This helps you with:

- grammar
- vocabulary
- pronunciation
- Practical English
- listening
- reading
- writing
- spelling

Keep a record of what you've done with the
Study Link Learning Record.

File 1 Study Link learning record

Workbook

		date
1A	✓	
1B	☑	10 October
1C	☑	24 October
1D	☐	
Practical English	☐	

MultiROM

- Grammar Quiz 1
- Vocabulary Banks ☐
  Numbers
  Countries and nationalities ☐
  Common objects ☐
- Practical English 1 ☐
- Audio – Workbook Question times 1A–D ☐

Website www.oup.com/elt/englishfile
- Grammar – File 1
- ☐

OXFORD
UNIVERSITY PRESS

Great Clarendon Street, Oxford OX2 6DP

Oxford University Press is a department of the University of Oxford.
It furthers the University's objective of excellence in research, scholarship,
and education by publishing worldwide in

Oxford New York

Auckland Cape Town Dar es Salaam Hong Kong Karachi
Kuala Lumpur Madrid Melbourne Mexico City Nairobi
New Delhi Shanghai Taipei Toronto

With offices in

Argentina Austria Brazil Chile Czech Republic France Greece
Guatemala Hungary Italy Japan Poland Portugal Singapore
South Korea Switzerland Thailand Turkey Ukraine Vietnam

OXFORD and OXFORD ENGLISH are registered trade marks of
Oxford University Press in the UK and in certain other countries

ISBN: 978 0 19 451828 4 Multipack
ISBN: 978 0 19 451829 1 Multibook

Printed in China

This book is printed on paper from certified and well-managed sources.

ACKNOWLEDGEMENTS

Design and composition by: Stephen Strong

*The authors would like to thank all the teachers and students round the world whose
feedback has helped us to shape New English File. We would also like to thank*: Qarie
and Victoria (Mark and Allie), Krysia for *Then he kissed me* and other ideas, all
our friends round the world who told us 'what made them feel good', and
Melissa for her interview. The authors would also like to thank all those at
Oxford University Press (both in Oxford and around the world), and the
design team.

Finally, very special thanks from Clive to Maria Angeles and Lucia, and from
Christina to Cristina for all their help and encouragement. Christina would
also like to thank her children Joaquin, Marco, and Krysia for their constant
inspiration.

*The Publisher and Authors would like to thank the following for their invaluable feedback
on the materials*: Beatriz Martin, Michael O'Brien, Lester Vaughan, Wendy
Armstrong, Javier Santos Asensi, Tim Banks, Brian Brennan, Susanna di
Gravio, Jane Hudson, Graham Rumbelow, and Krzysztof Wierzba.

*The authors and publisher are grateful to those who have given permission to reproduce
the following extracts and adaptations of copyright material*: p.63 'Kournikova of
chess makes her move' by Judith O'Reilly, *The Sunday Times* 31 March 2002.
Reproduced by permission of NI Syndication. p. 87 'First accident for 100-year
old motorist' by Gillian Harris, *The Times* 16 October 2001. Reproduced by
permission of NI Syndication. p.99 'Haile the Chief' by Paul Kimmage, *The
Sunday Times* 23 February 2003. Reproduced by permission of NI Syndication.
p.100 Extracts from 'This Life' by Roland White, *The Sunday Times*, 16
December 2001, 25 November 2001, 9 September 2001 and 21 November
1999. Reproduced by permission of NI Syndication. p.102 *Then he kissed me*
Words and Music by Phil Spector, Ellie Greenwich and Jeff Barry© 1963 by
Trio Music Co Inc, Mother Bertha Music Inc and Abkco Music Inc – All Rights
Reserved – Lyric reproduced by kind permission of Carlin Music Corp.,
London NW1 8BD.

Although every effort has been made to trace and contact copyright holders
before publication, this has not been possible in some cases. We apologize
for any apparent infringement of copyright and if notified, the publisher will
be pleased to rectify any errors or omissions at the earliest opportunity.

*The Publisher would like to thank the following for their kind permission to reproduce
photographs and other copyright material*: Action Images p.59 (Bayern Munich),
57 (RHPL/Sylvain Grandadam/girl on phone), 58 (Image State/Lee
Atherton/tennis, Aflo Foto Agency/rugby and cycling, Ace Stock
Ltd/basketball, Gai Wyn Williams/ aerobics), 66 (Nicholas
Pill/Travelsnaps/crocodile) 70 (Photofusion/Pete Jones), 82 (Mark Wood/biro),
85 (Cubolmages srl/Enzo Signorelli/Madonnina) Allstar p.55 (Cinetext/20th
Century Fox), 58 (volleyball), 73 (dancing), 79 (Kevork Djansezisn/Francis
Coppola), 80 (Mick Jagger), 79 (Yousuf Karsh of Ottowa/Hitchcock, Phil
Wilkinson/TSPL/Tarantino), 57 (M,ou Me Desjeux Bernard/Kraków), 73 (Galen
Rowell/mountains), 79 (Rufus F. Folkks/Sofia Coppola), FLPA p.151 (Mammal
Fund/ Earthviews/shark), Thomas England pp.94, 95, 59 (John
Peters/Manchester United), 66 (Getty Images (Darrell Gulin/bear), 82 (Image
Bank/dishwasher and windscreen wipers), 85 (RHPL/Tony Gervis/Duomo), 99
(Allsport), 151 (fly, National Georgraphic/whale), PW Henry p.63, Kobal
Collection pp.76 (20th Century Fox/Winona Ryder), 78 (Universal/The Birds,
A Band Apart/Miramax/Andrew Cooper/Kill Bill), Magnum p.109 and 113
(Marc Riboud/Eiffel Tower), NHPA p.151 (Stephen Dalton/mouse, Ernie
James/chicken, Kevin Schafer/goat, Harold Palo JR/mosquito, Ernie
James/horse, Daniel Zupanc/crocodile, Mike Lane/camel, John Shaw/butterfly,
wasp, Andy Rouse/cow and pig, duck, Martin Harvey/kangaroo, Patrick Fagot/
bull, rabbit, 58 (golf, judo), 67, 90, 106 (Hemera/jacket), 151 (Lion, sheep,
gorilla, eagle, bear, spider, elephant, tiger, swan), 61 (Ko Fujiwara/tennis),
Popperfoto p.82 (stockings), 61(Thai food), 82 (Photodisc Red/Ryan
McVay/nappies, tippex, Ingram Publishing/bullet proof vest, Photodisc
Green/Kim Steele/washing machine), 97 (Comstock/ food), 58 (baseball,
skiing, swimming), 66 (bull), 76 (Rupert Grint and Dennis Bergkamp), 80
(school photo), 82 (Dyson), 151 (dolphin and bee).

Illustrations by: Nick Baker pp.71, 137, 140, 142; Paul Dickinson p.102; Phil
Disley 52, 53, 64, 65, 67, 80, 88, 89, 92, 106; Mark Duffin p.48; Ellis Nadler
pronunciation symbols; Gary Kaye p.42, 68, 69; Jan McCafferty p.83; Colin
Shelbourn pp.58, 106, 152, 153; Colin Thompson pp.81, 87,100, 104, 105,
134, 139; Annabel Wright pp.54, 76, 77

Commissioned photography by: Mark Mason pp.60, 72, 84, 96, 97 (deckchair),
106 (t-shirt)

Picture research and illustrations commissioned by: Cathy Blackie

Thanks to: Paul Seligson and Carmen Dolz for the English Sounds Charts, pp.
156,158